SOMEWHERE IN ENGLAND

SOMEWHERE IN ENGLAND:
AMERICAN AIRMEN IN THE SECOND WORLD WAR

Edited by Jenny Cousins

Credits

Authors:

Jenny Cousins (ed.), Carl Warner, Lucy May Maxwell, Emily Charles, Sam Jolley,
Lucy Dale, Karina Flynn.

Acknowledgements:

Phil Jackson, Eric Burbridge, Roy Farrell, John Digby, Steve Woolford, Phillippa Wray, James
Rossington, Suzie Harrison, Tom Wrigglesworth, Stuart Hemsley, Jean Freeman, Norman Wells,
Paul Andrews, Ted Damick, Steve Ananian, Mark Copeland, Peter Randall, Gary Moncur, Keith
Ellefson, Paul Bellamy, Chris Brassfield, Lee Cunningham, David Osborne, Mike Osborn, Vivian
Rogers-Price, Nigel Julian, Geoff Rice, Jeff Hawley, Michael Faley, Debra Kujawa, Jason Webb,
Cory Goetsch, Amanda Reid-Cossentino, Theresa Jespersen.

Eighth Air Force Historical Society, Eighth in the East, National Museum of the Mighty Eighth Air
Force, Max Communications, the Heritage Lottery Fund, Bottisham Airfield Museum, Norfolk
& Suffolk Aviation Museum, Ashwell Village Museum.

Thanks also to Caitlin Flynn, Madeleine James, Abigail Lelliott, Georgia Davies, Leanne Hurren
and Kay Heather at IWM.

Published by IWM, Lambeth Road, London SE1 6HZ

iwm.org.uk

© The Trustees of the Imperial War Museum, 2015.

ISBN 978-1-904897-54-5

A catalogue record for this book is available from the British Library.

Printed and bound by Printer Trento

All images © IWM unless otherwise stated.

Every effort has been made to contact all copyright holders. The publishers will be glad to make
good in future editions any error or omissions brought to their attention.

10 9 8 7 6 5 4 3 2 1

INTRODUCTION

Over two million American servicemen passed through Britain during the Second World War. In 1944, at the height of activity, up to half a million were based there with the United States Army Air Forces (USAAF), most of them living in East Anglia. Their job was to man and maintain the vast fleets of aircraft needed to attack German cities and industry. Working with the Royal Air Force (RAF), the aim was to severely weaken Germany's ability to fight. It was a central part of the Allied strategy for winning the war, and absorbed vast resources in both the UK and the US. At the heart of the campaign were the bomber crews of the Eighth Air Force who flew through difficult conditions to drop their bombs deep within enemy territory. They were supported to and from the targets by fighter pilots who protected them from attack by enemy aircraft. When the Allies launched the campaign to liberate Europe in June 1944, the airmen of the Ninth Air Force played a vital role, carrying troops and attacking targets on the ground in support of the advancing armies.

Over 200 airfields were occupied or newly-built by the USAAF. Each one would house around 2,500 American men — many times the population of the nearest village. Thousands more GIs were based at smaller sites ('GI' was a common nickname for American soldiers and airmen and stood for 'Government issue' or 'General Issue'). American women served in many of these units, working for the American Red Cross or as members of the Women's Army Corps. Halls and country houses became headquarters for commanders and planners. Some were converted to hospitals or rest-homes for combat-weary fliers. Barns and outbuildings would house teams of truck drivers and their vehicles. Even specialist bakery units were dotted around the UK, providing fresh bread for the airmen. Captions on official press photographs kept locations secret, usually describing their subjects as being 'somewhere in England'.

No wonder, then, that their arrival was known as the 'friendly invasion': their impact on British life was huge. Villagers would count the aircraft out of their local base, and wait anxiously for their return. Children stood at the perimeter and made note of the aircraft that they saw. 'As an aeroplane-mad youth I was soon to relish the American presence in the East Anglian sky', recalled Roger Freeman, who grew up near Boxted airfield in Essex.

To British people familiar with Hollywood movies, the Americans were exciting and glamorous. They were well-dressed: their uniforms — the famous 'pinks and greens' — were of a higher quality than British equivalents. They were well-paid, especially compared to British troops, and many were generous with their cash and supplies — rare treats in rationed Britain. Some of them actually *were* film stars: it is difficult to overstate the excitement caused when people caught a glimpse of movie heroes such as Clark Gable or Jimmy Stewart in the local village pub.

There were tensions, of course. Many British people did not understand why African-American troops could not mix with white troops. 'I don't mind the Yanks, but I don't care much for the white fellows they've brought with them', was one (possibly apocryphal) quip. The phrase 'oversexed, overpaid and over here' summed up the frustrations that some — particularly British servicemen — felt about their American cousins. To deal with some of these criticisms, official guidance was issued on the history and cultural habits of both nations. 'Use common sense on all occasions', the guidance for US servicemen advised. 'By your conduct you have great power to bring about a better understanding between the two countries after the war is over. You will soon find yourself among a kindly, quiet, hardworking people who have been living under a strain such as few people in the world have ever known. In your dealings with them, let this be your slogan: It is always impolite to criticize your hosts; it is militarily stupid to criticize your allies.'

Most of the airmen were not much older than the children who were so fascinated by their arrival. For the majority, it was their first trip abroad. Some had never left their own state. From the moment they began training, they mixed with men from all over America, each one with different life experiences and expectations. Once in Britain, they behaved as tourists, taking photographs of their new friends and the places they visited. Many had British ancestors, and visited distant relatives or 'home' towns. Others were comforted by British families who provided them with a taste of the home life they had left behind.

Locally, airmen invested in maintaining good relations with their British friends. At Duxford in Cambridgeshire, seven youngsters who had lost parents were 'adopted' by the group. $400 was paid for each child for school and two meals a day for four years. The *Duxford Diary* noted that 'some units later added to this fund, for music lessons and other purposes. And whenever these or other kids came to the base, soldiers grabbed them up to entertain them. They knew they would have as much fun as the youngsters.'

Off-duty airmen teach American skills to British boys.

The Americans profoundly changed the places they inhabited. Their airfields were like 'little Americas', and the rich on-base culture seeped out into the surrounding areas. 'At one moment one is driving along a typical English country road, and the next, as if by magic, one is transported 3,000 miles across the Atlantic', wrote a journalist in *The Times*. Bands made of groups of musician-airmen toured the country. Locals were invited to base parties. 'I remember the Yanks almost more than I remember the war itself', said one Suffolk woman.

This bond between America and Britain that was forged in the Second World War is represented most strikingly by the tens of thousands of relationships that formed between American men and British women. Around 40,000 British 'GI brides' moved to America to start new lives with their American husbands. 'Our servicemen are marrying women who will be a credit to them wherever they go, and these marriages will undoubtedly contribute much toward favourable Anglo-American relations in the years ahead', wrote Duxford's Chaplain, Buford Fordham, in 1944.

In what is clearly a staged photograph for publicity purposes, American servicemen are treated to tea at a British home.

The majority of the Americans left Britain in 1945. Most went back to the United States, to the peacetime lives they had put on hold four years earlier. They left an enduring legacy. Their bases were only partly absorbed back into British rural communities. Runways were broken up and used for other construction projects. Buildings were re-used by farmers. Tools and equipment found their way into British garden sheds. Sometimes the airfields continued to be used for their designed purpose: London Stansted airport is a former USAAF base. Others found new roles as motor-racing circuits, turkey processing plants — even wind farms. Those which were ploughed back into the countryside are often easily identifiable as former airfields in aerial photographs, thanks to their unique shapes.

The names of the airfields – often shared with the nearby villages – became known far more widely because of their wartime associations. The names of villages such as Bassingbourn, Duxford, Thorpe Abbots, Grafton Underwood and a hundred more still resonate in towns and cities in America. For many families, these were the final places at which their loved ones lived.

The Americans are fondly remembered by those they met, especially the children they befriended who are now themselves grandparents. Hundreds of volunteers across East Anglia help preserve these memories. They look after memorials in village squares, on corners of former airfields, or at crash sites. They manage museums in former control towers, or preserve precious collections in pubs or farm buildings. They run websites and contribute to our growing interactive archive, americanairmuseum.com, helping present and future generations understand the enormous impact that these servicemen made.

One man did more than most to safeguard this legacy: Roger Freeman, the boy from Essex who was so fascinated by the base near where he grew up that it turned into a lifetime of research, writing and sharing. 'They were to leave a considerable impression on those who knew them, which did not easily fade when they departed', he wrote. Roger amassed thousands of photographs of this momentous period, a selection of which are presented in this book. The rest can be viewed on our online interactive archive.

For some families, photographs taken 'somewhere in England' were all that remained of their sons, husbands and fathers. Nearly 30,000 were killed flying from the UK during the Second World War. Some of them are buried at Cambridge American Cemetery, or are commemorated on its Wall of the Missing. Thanks to the generous support of its members, all are remembered in the American Air Museum, based at IWM Duxford, and it is to each one, and to all those who gave their service, that this book is dedicated.

ABOUT THE PHOTOGRAPHS

The photographs in this book have been selected from 15,000 in the Roger Freeman Collection, which Imperial War Museums (IWM) acquired for the nation in 2012.

Roger Anthony Wilson Freeman (1928–2005) grew up near Boxted airfield in Essex. The arrival of the Americans in 1943 marked the beginning of a lifelong interest. As a teenager, he took long bicycle rides to surrounding airfields and kept records of which aircraft were flying, who was flying them and what distinguishing marks (nose art and 'kills') were painted on them. When his mother took his jacket in to be cleaned, the owner of the shop found Roger's detailed notes in a pocket and called the police, sure that he had caught a German spy.

Roger Freeman investigates the site of a wartime P-51 Mustang crash at Leiston airfield in 1953.

Roger worked as a farmer all his life, but also found time to correspond with hundreds of American veterans and researchers in the USA and in Europe. The letters, official documents and photographs he amassed formed the basis of the more than 60 books he wrote about American airmen in Britain during the Second World War. His *Mighty Eighth* trilogy, published in the 1970s and 1980s, is still an essential resource for researchers.

Although a shy man, who preferred to collect photographs than to be in them, Freeman's expertise was called on by many different projects seeking historical accuracy. In 1989 he acted as the technical adviser on David Puttnam's *Memphis Belle* feature film and he assisted with the development of the American Air Museum, based at IWM Duxford, before its opening in 1997. He was also the historian of the Eighth Air Force Historical Society for many years.

The National Museum of the Mighty Eighth Air Force in Savannah, Georgia, collected some of Freeman's papers in 2005. Researchers looking at these records today work in a research centre named after Roger Freeman himself.

Freeman's detailed notes from 1944 include sketches of nose art.

Shortly before Roger died from a terminal illness, he decided to box up his study and sell the collection as a whole to his publishers. These same boxes were purchased by IWM in 2012 as part of a project to refresh the American Air Museum. For the next two years, the project team digitised and catalogued the 15,000 prints and slides that made up the photographic part of the collection. The vast majority of these photographs are now available on IWM's American Air Museum website. Launched in 2014, with the support of the Heritage Lottery Fund, the website seeks help from the public to caption the pictures, and acts as a repository for further material about the air war.

If you know something more about the people, aircraft and places depicted, or if you would like to try your hand at a bit of historical detective work, we would love you to go to americanairmuseum.com and add your stories to the archive.

Brigadier General Robert Candee of the USAAF shakes hands with Air Vice-Marshal John D'Albiac of the RAF as part of a ceremony to transfer an RAF airfield to the arriving Americans.

Both Candee and D'Albiac were lifelong military men with service records going back to the First World War. After graduating from Cornell in 1915, Candee served in the US Cavalry before transferring to the Air Service in 1922.

Like Candee, D'Albiac did not begin military life in the air force. Initially an officer in the British Army, he was seconded to the Royal Naval Air Service in 1915, where he served as an aeroplane observer, spotting German submarines off the French coast.

It was this sort of tactical air power that both men were responsible for in June 1943, when this photograph was taken. D'Albiac was in charge of the RAF's new 2nd Tactical Air Force, Candee the VIII Air Support Command, which would eventually become part of the US Ninth Air Force. Tactical air forces would play an important role in the success of Allied ground forces in north-west France the following year, when the push to liberate Europe from Nazi control intensified.

1st Lieutenant Immanuel 'Manny' Klette (third from the right) is snapped in a traditional crew photograph in front of his B-17 Flying Fortress 'Connecticut Yankee'.

As the pilot, Klette was in command of this 306th Bomb Group crew, but it would have taken all ten airmen working together to complete the 25 bombing missions tallied up on the aircraft's nose.

Beside Klette in the flight deck, the co-pilot shared the flying responsibilities. Below them in the nose the navigator directed the aircraft to its target and the bombardier released the bombs. Behind the pilots, the radio operator worked at a small desk, keeping the aircraft in contact if needed. The flight engineer was on hand to fix any mechanical problems that arose and to man the top turret gun.

The other four crew members protected the aircraft, manning guns in the waist, the ball turret suspended beneath the aircraft, and the tail.

Klette was one of the most respected pilots in the Eighth Air Force, flying 91 missions – a record for a bomber pilot in the European Theater of Operations (ETO).

Lieutenant Oswald Masoni with local girl, Barbara Deane, in front of his damaged aircraft.

A second-generation Italian from New York, Masoni flew as a navigator with the 379th Bomb Group at Kimbolton, Cambridgeshire.

Masoni was flying in the B-17 'Twentieth Century' (42-32000), returning from a mission to bomb Nazi-controlled airfields in Normandy, France, when flak (anti-aircraft fire) took out two of the engines. By the time the crew reached the Sussex coast, a third was failing and the captain chose to make a belly landing.

The aircraft crash-landed in Ethel Cheney's garden in Felpham, Sussex, just six feet from where she stood in her kitchen. Naturally she invited the entire crew in for tea.

As it was Independence Day and the final mission for the co-pilot, Lieutenant Mayo Adams, the crew set off all their flares in a ditch next to the house, bringing a slice of American culture to this small town. Twenty-five years later to the day, Mayo returned to have tea with Ethel again.

Captain Clark Gable talks to Sergeant Phil Hulse and Sergeant Kenneth Huls of the 351st Bomb Group. *(Overleaf)*

Clark Gable, star of *Gone With the Wind*, traded Hollywood glamour for military service in 1942. Dispatched to Polebrook, Northamptonshire, in April 1943 with a film crew of five, Gable produced and directed *Combat America*, which focused on the experience of aerial gunners. He flew on five missions in order to make the film.

Gable was not the only famous name involved with the USAAF in Britain. Actor Jimmy Stewart commanded a squadron, comedian Bob Hope and musician Glenn Miller entertained the troops, and Gable's *Gone With The Wind* co-star, Vivienne Leigh, also made official base tours.

Gable returned to the US to edit *Combat America*. The film was completed in 1944 and Kenneth Huls and Phil Hulse were both featured in the picture. Gable resumed his contract at MGM and once again became 'King of Hollywood', making films until his death in 1960.

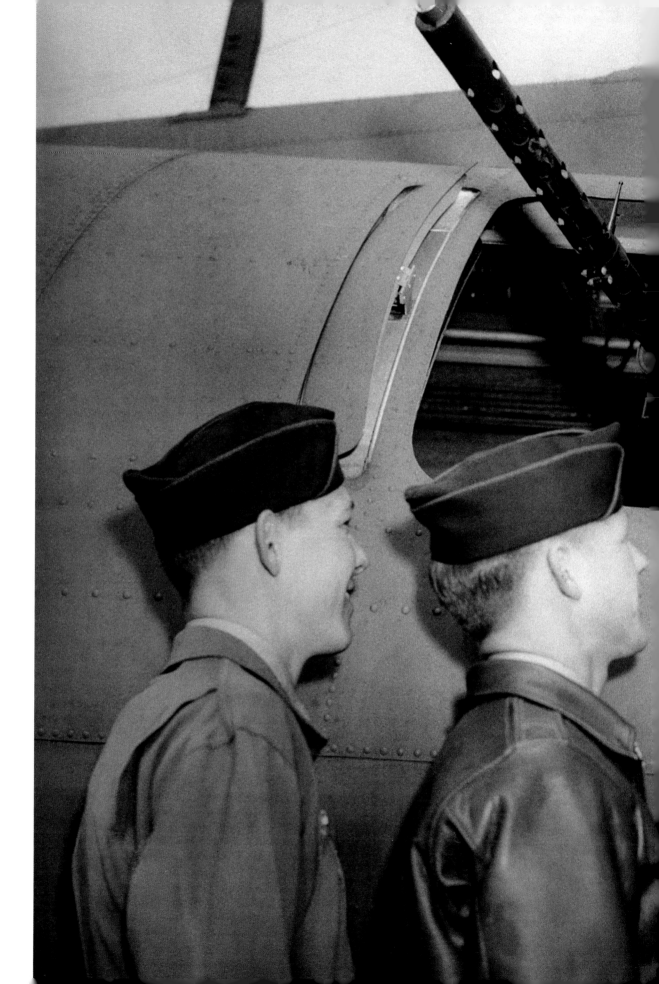

King George VI, Queen Elizabeth, Princess Elizabeth and Major General James 'Jimmy' Doolittle are introduced to Major Lloyd Mason of the 379th Bomb Group.

Based at Kimbolton, Cambridgeshire, the 379th Bomb Group hosted a visit from the royal family on 6 July 1944. The visiting party was also joined by a number of important USAAF officials, including Doolittle.

An itinerary was arranged for the royal party which included meeting crew members of B-17 Flying Fortress 'Four of a Kind', a base tour, and tea organised by the staff of the Red Cross Aero Club. Of particular delight to the hosts was the decision made by the royals to delay their onward journey so they could watch the 'Forts' land safely at Kimbolton after the day's mission to France.

The royal party then continued to Thurleigh in Bedfordshire, where the future Queen Elizabeth II christened an aircraft, named in her honour by the 306th Bomb Group as the 'Rose of York' (42-102547).

Hollywood director Major William Wyler (left) and British dramatist Terence Rattigan discuss the script of their planned film in front of a B-17 Flying Fortress.

Wyler was born in Alsace-Lorraine but emigrated to America aged 18 at the invitation of a producer cousin. He worked his way up the studio system to become one of Hollywood's most celebrated directors.

Wyler saw a role for himself in making pictures to support the war effort. He directed the most famous contemporary documentary about the air war, *Memphis Belle*. His *Mrs Miniver*, made prior to America's entry in the war, expressed strong sympathy with the fight against Nazism, and was described by Churchill as 'propaganda worth a hundred battleships'.

Rattigan is now well-known for his plays about English middle-class life. He joined the RAF as a gunner, flying maritime patrols, but following the success of his *Flare Path* in London's West End, he joined the No.1 Film Production Unit.

Although Wyler and Rattigan did not finish the collaboration which is captured in this photograph, the germ of the idea – a film about the close relationship between the USAAF and the RAF – eventually fed into the 1945 film *The Way to the Stars*.

Major Jesse Davis of the 78th Fighter Group is photographed with a local Duxford girl.

The US and UK authorities recognised the importance of maintaining good relations between the American military and their British hosts. Official guidance was issued on the history and cultural habits of both nations to encourage mutual respect and understanding. On a local level, efforts often focused on children, with bases holding Christmas parties and open days for nearby residents.

Davis, of Beloit, Wisconsin, joined the Army Air Corps in 1940. He arrived at Duxford in April 1943, and by June was commanding the 83rd Fighter Squadron. He would go on to fly 88 missions in P-47 Thunderbolts, and be awarded the Distinguished Flying Cross (DFC).

After the war, Davis was stationed in Germany and Japan, and spent five years as a professor of air science and tactics at the University of North Dakota. By 1964, he had been promoted to Lieutenant Colonel, and lived in Redlands, California, with his wife Christiana. In October of that year, with divorce pending, Davis murdered his wife and then killed himself.

Thirteen-year-old Peter Brame, laundry boy for the 95th Bomb Group, at Horham, Suffolk, August 1944.

Local women often did laundry for nearby air bases. Peter Brame's mother had an agreement with 1st Lieutenant George Dancisin's crew of the 412th Bomb Squadron, allowing Peter to act as their delivery boy in return for chocolate.

Here Peter stands in his Sunday best, proudly wearing a gifted pair of American wings. The photograph was taken by Lieutenant Albert Keeler, a co-pilot of the 95th Bomb Group who took many pictures around the base.

American air bases in Britain often attracted the attention of local children who found the aircraft and Americans exciting. For those whose own fathers were away on service, the Americans provided a male source of affection and some children became like mascots to the servicemen. Under the strictures of wartime rationing, American candy was also particularly appealing.

Janet Townshend and sisters Tessa and Gloria Grant help the 466th Bomb Group celebrate the milestone of 100 combat missions at Attlebridge, Norfolk, August 1944.

They are holding a weather balloon, which has been marked for the occasion. Glen Miller and his orchestra were flown in, and other special guests included Rudy Starita's 'All Girl Orchestra' and Hollywood film star Lieutenant Colonel Jimmy Stewart.

Press photographers were there to record the event. The *New York Times* reported that 'the men had a great day – movie shows, ball games, and pony trotting with bookmakers were some of the attractions'.

An estimated 10,000 people in total were on base that day, including many local British residents. Janet, Tessa and Gloria came from nearby Hockering. The Grant sisters' cousin, Keith Bailey, lived on a farm in Weston Longville, which bordered the base. Keith's son John identified the Grant sisters when we posted this photograph online.

Margaret Holley, nee Scott, and her bridesmaids Phyllis, Iris and Mary, July 1945. *(Overleaf)*

Margaret married Corporal Milton Holley of the 401st Bomb Group, based at Deenethorpe in Northamptonshire. Ten months after their marriage, Margaret sailed for New York with 520 other 'GI brides' (and one GI baby) on SS *President Tyler*.

It was a huge step for the approximately 40,000 women who left the UK to make new lives in America, and not all war bride stories ended happily. Many had known their husbands for only a short time before they were sent back to America, and the relationships did not last. Sometimes the husbands got cold feet, and did not come to meet their wives when they arrived.

Happily, Milton and Margaret's marriage lasted for the rest of their lives. They settled in Michigan and raised a family, living in the house they built. Milton died in 2000 and Margaret passed away in 2002, aged 86.

William Glasscock and his daughter, Pearl, deliver meat from T D Dennis, a butcher's shop in Ashwell, Hertfordshire.

This photograph was taken by a USAAF airman, and may have been intended as a souvenir of what British rural life was like.

Captured here, brandishing a meat saw poised over a leg joint, is William Glasscock. Raised on his family's farm before it folded, Glasscock became a delivery boy for T D Dennis as a teenager. During the war, he joined his local Home Guard unit and like 1.5 million other men too old or young for military service, spent his Sundays training to be the last line of defence in the event of a German invasion.

Glasscock's teenage daughter, Pearl, worked beside him on his deliveries and his youngest son, Roger, would later work in the grocery shop next to T D Dennis.

Jan Houston Monaghan is delighted to find fresh fruit on offer at a VE Day garden party near her base at Wormingford, Essex.

As an American Red Cross 'doughnut girl' she dished out doughnuts and coffee to the mechanics as they worked to keep the aircraft in flying condition. Robert Sand (pictured on page 126), the airman who photographed her, recalled 'how welcome was the hot coffee on those icy days'.

Jan's memories of her service include her battle against the dogs which would come into the Red Cross club and sleep on the chairs, making the upholstery dirty. She recalled that whenever the club announced that unregistered dogs would be put to sleep, 'every guy would hasten to adopt a dog and have it registered. The dog population grew and grew and I fought a losing battle with the chairs.'

While in England, Jan Houston met and married Sergeant John 'Jack' Monaghan of the 55th Fighter Group. After the war she continued to provide support to those who needed it in her local community. Among the many charitable causes she worked for over the decades were Habitat for Humanity, which builds homes for low-income families, and her church's AIDS care team.

Corporal Joseph Sleeping Bear (left) is pictured with a colleague serving Thanksgiving dinner to school children at Snetterton Heath, Norfolk, November 1944.

Sleeping Bear grew up in Running Bird township, an Indian reservation in South Dakota. He belonged to the Sioux tribe.

No section of American society that participated in the Second World War made a greater per capita contribution than the Native Americans. An estimated 44,000 in a population of 350,000 signed up to the military.

Sleeping Bear began his service in 1943, joining the 96th Bomb Group at Snetterton Heath. It was common for American bases to host local children, especially orphans, during the holiday season. Rationing meant that items in the feast being enjoyed at this table were in short supply – the ordinary weekly allowance of butter and cheese was just 2 oz (50g) per person.

After the war, Sleeping Bear returned to Mellette, South Dakota, where he married Violet Landeaux in 1958.

Left to right: 1st Lieutenant Stanley Markusen, Major Charles Clapp Jr, William Randolph Hearst Jr and Major John DuFour, watch a mission take-off at Duxford.

The USAAF kept up an extensive programme of public relations, with good news stories to help build the service's profile at home, encourage recruitment and maintain morale amongst servicemen.

Markusen was public relations officer at Duxford and Clapp headed VIII Fighter Command's public relations section. Their duties included releasing information to the newspapers and receiving VIPs. Here they are hosting the son of the famous and influential newspaper owner, William Randolph Hearst.

Although this photograph was taken in 1943, fighter pilot John DuFour was already a veteran of over 100 missions to Europe. He had been part of one of the Eagle Squadrons – RAF units formed from American volunteers who came to take part in the fight against Nazism before America's official entry into the war.

39

Captain Frederick Christensen Jr with his P-47 Thunderbolt, July 1944.

Fred Christensen had long desired to be a fighter pilot. The son of Norwegian immigrants, he joined the USAAF in 1942 following the German invasion of Norway. He was assigned to the 56th Fighter Group, known as the 'Wolfpack'.

With 21.5 victories to his name (half a kill was credited when it was impossible to work out who fired the critical shot), Christensen was the seventh highest-scoring fighter ace in the Eighth Air Force.

At the time of this photograph, Christensen held the record for the highest number of enemy aircraft shot down in a single combat mission. On 7 July 1944, he braved heavy flak to shoot down six German transport aircraft near Gardelegen, Germany, in less than two minutes. 'There really was nothing much to it', he said to a war correspondent on his return.

Christensen attributed some of his success to his lucky charm – a stray black cat named Sinbad whom he had adopted and reportedly took flying. They both returned to the US in 1944, after completing 107 missions. Christensen continued to fly with the Massachusetts Air National Guard until 1971. He died in 2006.

Lieutenant Edwin Wright of the 404th Fighter Group, shows off the damage to his P-47 Thunderbolt, October 1944.

Wright belonged to the Ninth Air Force, which, following the ground invasion in June 1944, moved its bases from Britain to mainland Europe in order to provide closer support to the advancing troops. This picture was taken near St Trond, Belgium.

It was not the first time Wright's aircraft had been hit on a mission. By the time this photograph was taken, the 19-year-old had completed 39 missions and survived being hit by flak six times.

Wright was considered a very fortunate man by his squadron, who nicknamed him 'Lucky', for his ability to evade death. The hole here measured 8 inches in diameter in an 11-inch propeller. If the damage had been an inch and a half over on either side, the blade would have severed and Wright would have been brought down.

Wright died, aged 34, from lung cancer.

Staff Sergeant Richard Grimm of the 303rd Bomb Group,
pictured in his flying gear.

Grimm was a radio operator and flew 35 missions. His first, aged 19,
was a smooth run to Herøya, Norway, and back. His second was a very
different affair.

Heading for Hamburg, Germany, Grimm took position in the ball turret after
the gunner felt sick. The aircraft was flying at a high altitude and Grimm failed
to hook up to its oxygen and heating systems before his own supply ran out.
He fell unconscious and, noticing him freezing to death down in the turret,
the ball turret gunner desperately tried to get him out as the other crew
members fought off German attackers.

When they were through the worst of it, three of them managed to pull
Grimm out and revive him. 2nd Lieutenant Raymond Cassidy said later
that Grimm had 'been out for 45 minutes and I thought sure he was dead'.

Grimm went on to fly 25 missions with the Air Rescue Service during
the Korean War. After retiring from the USAAF in 1954, he worked as an
electrical engineer for Raytheon, specialising in radar and communication
and control systems.

Bombardier, Lieutenant Harry Erickson of the 97th Bomb Group,
in the nose of a B-17 Flying Fortress, July 1942.

As bombardier, Erickson occupied the glass cabin in the B-17's nose. It was
his job to release bombs accurately over the target, using the top-secret
Norden bombsight device. The Norden helped the bombardier to make
complex calculations, but it needed near-perfect conditions to work,
including good weather, which proved elusive. American aircraft
eventually also used electronic devices, similar to those used by RAF crews.

The son of a steam railroad engineer from Mankato, Minnesota, Erickson
only completed eight missions. In October 1942, his friend Lieutenant Ben
Rushing recorded in his journal, 'Erickson was lost. He went in someone
else's plane and happened to [have] hard luck. You begin to realize that
it is war when they get your best buddies ... I can hardly realize that he is
definitely lost ... May his soul rest in peace.'

However Erickson did not die; he was captured and became a prisoner
of war for nearly three years.

Radio Operator, Technical Sergeant Robert Siavage, at his station on board a B-17 Flying Fortress, January 1943.

As radio operator, Siavage's main job was to communicate with the base and other aircraft. He would also have been responsible for photographing the bomb run to determine its effectiveness, as well as performing first aid and manning a gun if necessary.

The son of a Polish coal miner, Siavage came from Pennsylvania. He belonged to the 306th Bomb Group, based at Thurleigh in Bedfordshire, and was in the first B-17 to bomb Germany on 27 January 1943. The US Eighth Air Force began flying missions from the UK in mid-1942, focusing on targets in occupied Europe, particularly in France. It carried out 31 missions during 1942, compared with 118 missions in 1943 and 256 missions in 1944 at the height of its strength, dropping to 85 missions in the final year of the war.

Two months after this photograph was taken, Siavage's aircraft was shot down. He bailed out and was captured and sent to Stalag 17b in Austria, where he spent the next two years as a prisoner of war.

Staff Sergeant Ward Kirkpatrick gets into a ball turret on a B-17 Flying Fortress, April 1943.

Kirkpatrick came from Montana, where he worked for his father's construction firm. He was assigned to the 303rd Bomb Group, which operated from Molesworth in Cambridgeshire.

As a ball turret gunner, he had to look out for enemy aircraft approaching from all angles – he could rotate 360 degrees horizontally and up to 90 degrees vertically. The ball turret gunner was often considered the most dangerous position on a B-17 because it appeared so exposed. However, the cramped space meant that its occupant presented the smallest possible target area to flak and enemy fighters.

Kirkpatrick was shot down a month after this photo was taken. All of the crew were killed. He is listed on the Wall of the Missing in the Cambridge American Cemetery as his body was never found. As was the normal procedure in such cases, his family was initially told he was missing in action and death was confirmed seven years later.

Staff Sergeant Richard 'Slug' Schultheis in the waist of a B-17 Flying Fortress. (Overleaf)

According to a contemporary survey, 86% of casualties were a result of flak, anti-aircraft fire from the ground.

Waist gunners stood, meaning that their whole bodies were exposed. There was very little protection from the thin metal aircraft skin. They would often take a pair of flak jackets with them, one to wear and one to stand on to provide a small amount of extra protection from flak bursting up through the floor.

Schultheis served as a waist gunner in the 385th Bomb Group. He enlisted in 1942 and completed 35 missions. After sustaining a head wound, he returned to Pennsylvania and spent the rest of his life working for a steel company.

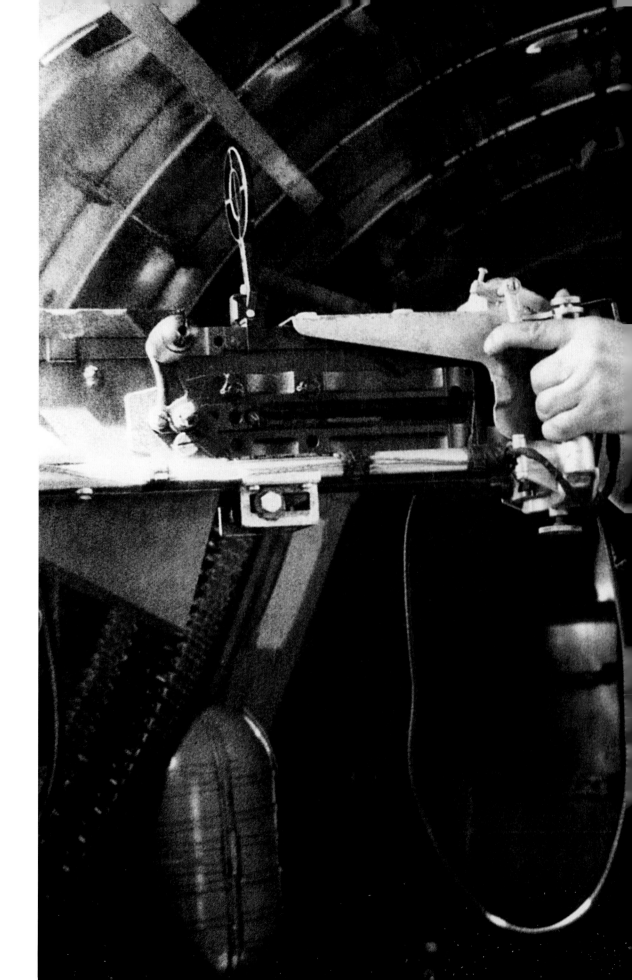

Sergeant Leo Teetman Jr celebrates New Year's Eve, 1943,
with a post-mission sandwich and coffee.

Leo Teetman was born in Brooklyn, New York, to parents of Polish descent,
and lived most of his life on the East Coast. He joined up in 1942 and
was assigned as a gunner to the 384th Bomb Group, based at Grafton
Underwood in Northamptonshire.

Teetman completed 25 missions in the early stage of the bombing campaign,
when the Eighth Air Force's focus was on occupied Europe. This photograph
was taken after returning from an attempt to target a ship in the mouth of the
Garonne River in southern France. The weather was terrible and forced several
of the bombers to land away from home. In this picture, Leo is at Kimbolton,
Cambridgeshire, an airfield which lies around 20 miles distant from his
own base. It was his first mission, and he was 20 years old.

Teetman settled in Connecticut, where he worked for a company
making optical instruments. He married and had three children.

Staff Sergeant Jayson Smart of the 305th Bomb Group, immediately
after a mission, August 1943.

A splinter cut his brow during the mission, and blood has streaked his face
in the shape of his oxygen mask.

From Branchport, New York, Smart enlisted in August 1942. He was 20 years
old and already married, to Arlene.

The day this photograph was taken, Smart had flown as a waist gunner
on the B-17 'Big Bust' on a mission to the Ruhr Valley in Germany. This
was the first daylight operation to the Ruhr, which had acquired the
grimly humorous moniker 'Happy Valley' due to the scale of German
defences which protected its heavy industry.

The bombers flew unescorted by fighter aircraft, and were badly scattered
en route. Enemy fighter opposition and flak damaged 15 of the 20 bombers
from the 305th Bomb Group. Ten other men from the group were wounded
and a further ten were missing in action. 83 men from the whole formation
were killed in action.

Major General Carl Spaatz, commanding general of the USAAF in the European Theater, pins the Distinguished Service Cross on Major Charles Kegelman.

Next to Kegelman is 2nd Lieutenant Randall Dorton, Sergeant Robert Golay and Sergeant Bennie Cunningham. The four American airmen had flown with RAF bombers on a mission over Holland on 4 July 1942. This was reported back home as the first official mission of the Eighth Air Force, timed to coincide with Independence Day.

Their aircraft had come under heavy fire and one propeller had been shot away. Kegelman had managed to keep the bomber in the air and the crew had been able to hit the German airfield and make it back to base. The second American crew who flew to the same target were shot down, with three crew members killed.

Sergeant Golay described getting home in *Yank* magazine: 'They had a whole bottle of Scotch waiting for us. You don't know what that means over there. Why, you have to walk twenty miles just for a glass of beer alone.'

Red Cross Aero Club manager Lucille Parker inside a B-17 Flying Fortress, November 1943.

The American Red Cross had been asked by the US Armed Forces to provide recreational services for their men. Lucille Parker, from New York City, managed the Red Cross Aero Club at Molesworth, Cambridgeshire. She established the club with fellow New Yorker, Adelaide Noaks, in April 1943.

Parker, previously a pilot in the Civilian Air Patrol, had accrued 1,600 flying hours and made 189 parachute jumps. She had more experience than some of the young airmen frequenting her club, and would deliver informal talks about bailing out. In 1944, the *Brooklyn Eagle* newspaper praised her work: 'She helps them get over the fears that even the bravest men admit.'

Parker's daily duties included darning socks and serving coffee. In 1943, with the assistance of station chaplain Edmund Skoner (pictured on page 86), she helped to organise a Christmas party for local children, for which Santa Claus was specially transported from the North Pole inside a B-17 bomber.

Corporal George Oelkers picks up the wings of a butterfly bomb, dropped by a German aircraft the previous night in an attack on Parham airfield.

Parham was the target of several of these opportunistic raids, as it was only ten miles from the Norfolk coast.

Oelkers was part of the 390th Bomb Group's ordnance staff, which coordinated the 'bombing-up' of aircraft and supplied small arms ammunition for the guns. The ordnance men had to work together well and handle the equipment carefully at all times to prevent accidents occurring from bombs exploding unintentionally. Signs along the road to the ammunition dump read 'Remember Alconbury', 'Remember Rattlesden', 'Remember Ridgewell' and 'Remember Metfield', where accidents had occured.

At the end of the war Oelkers returned home to New Jersey and worked for many years as a jewellery manufacturer for Krementz and Co., a successful Newark firm.

Lieutenant Gustave Binnebose (left) and Chief Aviation Pilot James Chandler of Fleet Air Wing 7 of the US Navy, inside the cockpit of their PB4Y-1 (a modified B-24). *(Overleaf)*

Binnebose and Chandler flew from Dunkeswell in Devon, which was transferred to the US Navy in 1943 and remained the only US naval air base on British soil. Fleet Air Wing 7 carried out anti-submarine patrols in the Western Atlantic and the Bay of Biscay. Crews were forced to fly 'low and slow', removing any margin for error and rendering parachutes redundant.

In February 1944, Binnebose, Chandler and their crew were joined aboard their aircraft, 'B is for Baker', by Bud Hutton, Chief Air Force Correspondent for *Stars and Stripes* magazine. He revealed how the navigator would announce their distance from England, allowing the crew to calculate how far they were from home. This particular mission coincided with Chandler's birthday – 'as good a way as any' to turn 23, he said.

Staff Sergeant Elmer Leonard in front of a B-17, with his souvenirs from a shuttle mission.

Shuttle missions allowed bombers to fly to the limits of their range, refuel and rearm in Allied territory – either the Soviet Union or North Africa – and then bomb a further target on the return.

Leonard, from Maine, was a top turret gunner in the 390th Bomb Group, based at Parham in Suffolk. On 17 August 1943, he was credited with shooting down a Messerschmitt on a shuttle mission attacking German factories in Regensburg and Schweinfurt. After refuelling in North Africa his crew returned to the UK, where he was photographed with some of the souvenirs they brought back: the nose of a Heinkel, a German machine gun and a fez.

Two months later, Leonard was shot down on a mission to Münster, Germany. He was imprisoned in Stalag Luft III in east Germany, where he remained until January 1945. Along with many others, he was force-marched under extremely harsh conditions to Nuremberg, and later Moosberg, by German guards keen to avoid the advancing Russians. He was liberated in April 1945.

Leonard died in 2004, the founder of E W Leonard Inc., a heating and engineering systems company in Maine and Connecticut.

Virginia Irwin, features writer from the *St Louis Post-Dispatch*, interviews Lieutenant Glennon 'Bubbles' Moran of the 352nd Fighter Group.

Irwin joined the *St Louis Post-Dispatch* newspaper in 1932. Her request to be sent abroad to cover the war was denied, but in 1943 she volunteered to work for the Red Cross on an air base in the UK.

Just before D-Day, Irwin's paper changed its mind. Conveniently close to the action, she was accredited as an official war correspondent and reported on progress in 1944 and 1945 as the Allies pushed east towards Germany. This photograph was taken during an interview with Moran, a fighter ace who would continue his air force career in Korea and the Cold War, retiring as a Brigadier General. There is a bridge named after him in Missouri.

The scoop of Irwin's career came when she and another journalist drove through Russian lines to Berlin, arriving on 27 April 1945. It was four days before Hitler's suicide and the city was in chaos. Held back until Germany's official surrender, her stories later became headline news. Irwin was awarded a year's salary as a bonus, but on returning home she was assigned back to the features department. She never succeeded in breaking into the all-male newsroom.

An unknown African-American airman poses with the nose art of the B-24 Liberator 'Full House', 1944.

Nothing is known about this airman beyond what can be seen in the photograph: he wears a wedding ring and at least one front tooth is missing. However he would probably have been part of the Eighth Air Force's Combat Support Wing, which was established in 1943 to unite ordnance, transport and engineering units and build their morale.

Personnel from the Combat Support Wing would deliver bombs to the air bases. This B-24 was located with the 44th Bomb Group at Shipdham, Norfolk, in 1944. Nearby bases, where this airman could have been stationed, include Eye, Debach and Haughley Park.

His anonymity is indicative of the status of African-American servicemen. Although the 'Tuskegee Airmen' flew in the Mediterranean, African-Americans were barred from combat roles in the Eighth Air Force and could not serve in units with white men. While relations with the British locals were generally cordial, segregation was sometimes effectively applied by the military — pubs and even whole villages could be designated for use by one particular race on certain nights of the week.

As one serviceman commented after the war, 'we black troops went overseas to fight the Germans, but we had to fight the Yanks first'.

Technical Sergeant Lester Reifeiss (left) and Sergeant Jasper
'J D' Taylor of the 78th Fighter Group repair a P-47 Thunderbolt
at Duxford, Cambridgeshire.

Ground crews were responsible for the routine maintenance of aircraft.
They included general mechanics and specialists who repaired particular
parts, such as instruments or armour. Servicing had to be regular and
painstakingly thorough in order to keep equipment battle-ready and safe.
The job could be both monotonous and highly-pressured, with work going
on around the clock. A ground crew generally worked on the same aircraft
and might feel a sense of ownership for it, just as an air crew often did.

Reifeiss came from Missouri, and Taylor from Oklahoma. Like many young
men in the army, they probably had not travelled outside of their home
state before the war, and would have been expected to live similar lives
to their fathers. Reifeiss had just begun to work as an office clerk for a
wholesale hardware firm like his father Otto, and Taylor was employed
on the family farm.

British worker Jim Robson inspects the results of his handiwork up close.

Robson worked for British Indestructo Glass, which manufactured laminated safety glass for bombers' ball turrets.

American airmen from the 303rd Bomb Group had previously visited the factory to see how the innovative layered glass was made. Jim's name was picked out of a ballot to be the British worker who made the return visit to Molesworth airfield in Cambridgeshire.

Earlier in life, Jim had been a miner in County Durham but during the war he worked in London making glass. His job involved layering transparent plastic between cut plates of glass, which made the glass safer as it could no longer shatter.

It is not known what employment Jim Robson took after the war. However for British Indestructo Glass, the post-war world was a hard one and, after years of financial difficulties, it was merged with Triplex Safety Glass Company Limited in 1967. Its London factory was closed and several hundred workers were made redundant.

Warrant Officer Cecil Broxton
with an empty 'drop tank'.

Fighter aircraft were fitted with auxiliary
fuel tanks made from a very light
pressed-paper composite to enable them
to escort bombers further into Germany.

As a warrant officer, Cecil could have been
responsible for all of the fuel stores on base.
It was the highest non-commissioned rank
in the USAAF and came with a high level
of responsibility.

Cecil grew up in a large farming family
in Alabama. Both he and his brother,
Howell, joined the US Army in the 1930s
and served through the Korean War into
the 1960s. Howell flew as a fighter pilot
with the 356th Fighter Group from
Martlesham Heath in Suffolk. The two
brothers met up in October 1944, soon after
Howell had successfully evaded capture in
Holland. He was back in the USA by late 1944.
Cecil, as a ground officer, could not complete
a tour of duty in the same way as a flying
officer could. It is likely that he remained
in England until his unit left altogether.

Intelligence Officer Captain Gordon Burris explains a model he has developed to help pilots visualise formations of bombers and fighters over different altitudes, December 1943.

Intelligence officers like Burris were responsible for briefing crews before their missions and interrogating them when they returned. The information he collected went towards assembling a fuller picture of the impact of the air war, and determining where and how to strike next. Burris was part of the Ninth Air Force's 354th Fighter Group, based at Boxted in Essex, when this photograph was taken. The Ninth's role was to support the ground invasion to liberate Europe by destroying targets on or near the front line.

Burris's model shows how fighter aircraft were used to protect bomber aircraft by flying above and behind, ready to defend them from German Luftwaffe fighters. The bombers are on the bottom two levels.

Before the war, Burris was a municipal court judge in Canton, Ohio, and dealt with the kinds of cases that would be heard by a magistrate in the UK. Soon after returning home, he married, spending his three-week honeymoon in Florida.

Captain Jesse Barrett Jr contemplates a model of a German Heinkel He 111.

Bomber crews attended classes on aircraft recognition as part of their training for being under fire. As a Group Intelligence Officer for the 303rd Bomb Group, Barrett also spoke to crews after they returned from a mission in order to prepare Missing Air Crew Reports (MACRs). These reports ascertained which of the group's aircraft had failed to return and recorded the probable fates of crew members.

Over the course of his service, Barrett flew as an observer on ten combat missions over Occupied Europe. For this he was awarded an Air Medal with oak leaf cluster, rare for a 'ground pounder'. He would have been hoping to familiarise himself with the customs of aerial combat, to better prepare MACRs, and perhaps to catch sight of the latest modifications to Luftwaffe aircraft. Combat experience would also perhaps have earned him the respect of crews he briefed before a mission and asked tough questions of afterwards.

Major General Ira Eaker poses beside a map showing recent bombing targets hit by American bombers flying from Britain, August 1943.

Eaker was the commanding general of the Eighth Air Force. He had pushed for American bombers to fly daylight bombing raids rather than join the RAF on night-time raids. He believed that by flying during the day American bombers would be able to strike German industrial targets more effectively. In a memo that made it into the hands of British Prime Minister Winston Churchill he added, 'we shall bomb them round the clock and the devil shall get no rest'. Churchill was convinced and this round-the-clock bombing by the Allied air forces became known as the Combined Bomber Offensive. It was thought that the position of the Nazis on the continent could be significantly weakened by destroying the industrial sites they relied on to build and maintain their armed forces.

The daylight bombing campaign achieved mixed results. Thick cloud was prone to completely obscure targets and bombardiers had trouble releasing bomb-loads accurately. Eaker stated after the war that, 'if we had not had strategic bombing ... perhaps a million men would have died that lived through that struggle'.

Lieutenant John Gerber smokes his pipe during a briefing for pilots of the 2nd Scouting Force. Noticeboards in the background have been partially obscured by the censor.

Gerber studied at the University of Colorado before enlisting in Denver in October 1942. He served as a pilot of the 56th Fighter Group, based at Halesworth, Suffolk, and later the 2nd Scouting Force, stationed at Steeple Morden, Cambridgeshire. He flew both P-47 Thunderbolts and P-51 Mustangs during his service.

As a scouting pilot, Gerber's job was to lead the bomber crews through bad weather to their targets. He would have evaluated weather conditions for the mission commander and helped to tighten and defend the bomber formations as they travelled over Europe.

Following the war, Gerber returned to the University of Colorado. He completed graduate studies in aerospace engineering while simultaneously serving as a pilot in the Colorado Air National Guard. After graduating, he went on to work with Lockheed Aerospace. His passion for flight never left him and he ultimately built and flew his own replica Spitfire.

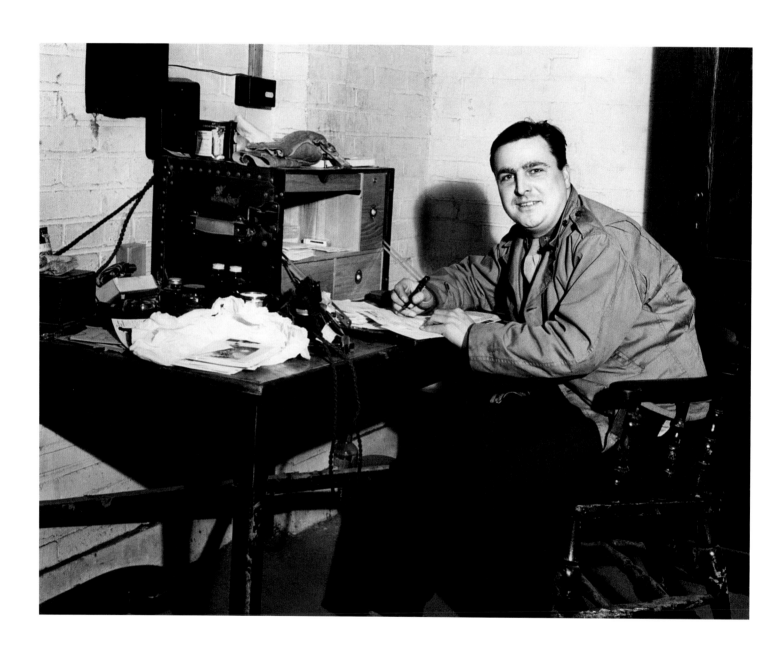

Captain Edmund Skoner, chaplain, sits at his desk at Molesworth air base, Cambridgeshire, December 1942.

Skoner was attached to the 303rd Bomb Group, known as the 'Hell's Angels'. One of his duties was to write letters of condolence to the families of missing or killed airmen. When this photograph was taken, the 303rd had only flown six of their eventual 364 missions, with the loss of three B-17s. Skoner's work was only just beginning. By the war's end, the 303rd had suffered 1,764 casualties (killed or missing in action and prisoners of war) out of 8,960 serving men.

Chaplains might themselves be Protestant, Jewish or, in Skoner's case, Catholic, but it was their responsibility to provide spiritual guidance for all faiths. They also helped maintain morale and encouraged good relations with the local population. Skoner would have conducted services and arranged alternative local worship for the men he could not minister to himself. Before joining up, he was assistant priest at the Immaculate Conception Catholic Church in Chicago. He returned there after the war and eventually retired to Florida.

Sergeant Jose 'Joe' Dominguez of the 1773rd Ordnance Supply and Maintenance Company, based at Kimbolton, Cambridgeshire, holds food he has prepared in his role as Colonel Maurice Preston's cook.

Food could be a heated topic for American servicemen in Britain. While American bases were generally better catered than British, GIs could not escape the tyranny of British wartime vegetables, Brussels sprouts in particular. A brief respite came to airmen on the morning before a mission, when they were given fresh eggs (dubbed 'combat eggs') in place of the usual powdered variety ('square eggs').

US authorities became concerned that the British wartime diet was hindering American morale in Britain, so 32% of food was shipped in from the States. Among these supplies was peanut butter, which one sergeant jokingly claimed 'saved our lives'.

In choosing Joe Dominguez as his personal cook, Colonel Maurice Preston had a better chance than many to get good food on his plate. Dominguez had followed his stepfather into the restaurant business in Santa Fe, New Mexico. Moving to Los Angeles, he had worked as a cook in the commissary kitchen at Warner Bros. Studios and at Hollywood's world-famous Brown Derby restaurant. Colonel Preston flew 45 combat missions, many of which may have started with Dominguez's 'combat eggs'.

Captain George 'Doc' Hornig, flight surgeon of the 56th Fighter Group, prepares medicine, November 1943.

Doc was responsible for the wellbeing of the pilots he worked with, administering medicine and conducting health checks to keep them flying. His care extended to making the pilots coffee on their return from missions, checking their oxygen equipment was functioning properly, even occasionally escorting their forbidden female visitors out of the base in his ambulance!

Doc was 'a combination of family physician, foster-father and chaplain to the pilots', according to a press photographer who shadowed him on his daily duties at Halesworth, Suffolk. 'To prepare for this, he studied aviation medicine – including psychology, psychiatry and plastic surgery.'

Doc returned to the United States in October 1945 with souvenirs of his time in Europe, including a Nazi flag and an SS sword. He worked at the North Country Community Hospital in Glen Cove, New York, and died aged 43 in June 1954.

Sergeant Leroy Nitschke, an armorer with the 4th Fighter Group, stands beside boxes of ammunition at Debden air base in Essex.

Nitschke was born in St Louis, Missouri, the son of a German cabinetmaker. He was a veteran of two wars and two services, having been in the US Navy in the First World War. As a civilian, he worked as an accountant at a telephone company. By the time the Second World War broke out, his father had died and he was living with his mother.

An armorer's job was to inspect and maintain aircraft-mounted guns, cannons and any related mechanisms. At 43 years old in 1942, he was twice the age of many of the men who operated the weapons he serviced. It is perhaps for this reason that he was known as 'Old Nick'.

After the war he helped set up a veterans association, which held its first reunion in 1968 and is still running today.

Sergeant Charles Lahey of the Medical Corps, carries a laundry bundle out of the officers' quarters at Molesworth air base, Cambridgeshire, 1942.

Being in the Medical Corps could have landed Lahey all kinds of jobs around base. The official press caption with this photograph reported that he'd said, 'Love to my parents and to all my friends back home. We'll keep 'em flying.' Lahey's father was an insurance salesman in Chicago. His mother was of German descent.

Lahey died on Christmas day in 1944. His body was recovered after a severe snowstorm at Molesworth. He is one of many men and women who died while serving in the armed forces from a cause that was not directly related to combat action. Several of the graves in the Cambridge American Cemetery at Madingley have similar stories behind them, although Lahey's body was repatriated to the USA after the war.

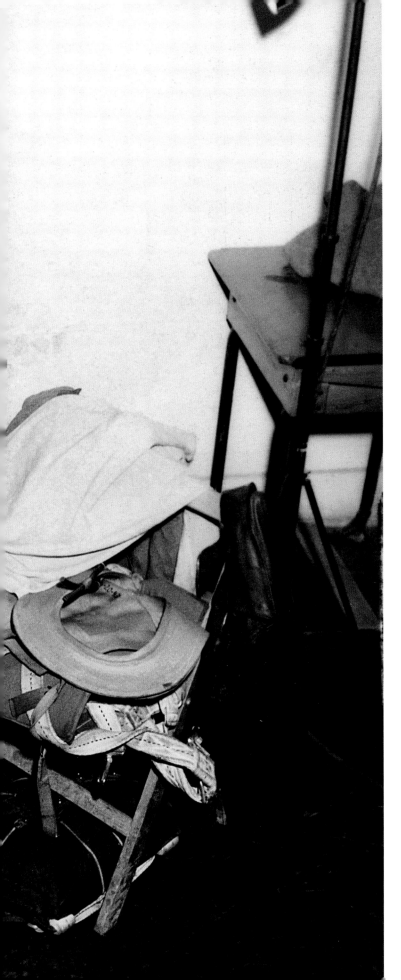

Staff Sergeant William Fleming poses for the first of a sequence of newspaper photographs.

Fleming was a waist gunner for the 303rd Bomb Group. This photograph was the first of several published in Indiana's *Alexandria Times-Tribune* in October 1943, showing Fleming dressing for a mission.

Bombers flew at a high altitude and temperatures could fall as low as -50°C. Keeping warm was of paramount importance. Frostbite was a major hazard which grounded over 1,500 men in one year alone. An airman's protective kit included an electrically-heated flying suit, a life jacket (dubbed 'Mae Wests' after the curvaceous film star), sheepskin boots, heated gloves, a flak jacket and a parachute worn over the top.

The equipment, however, was wholly unreliable and uncomfortable. The electric suits short-circuited easily and there were stories of life jackets inflating inside the aircraft, limiting movement and sometimes trapping crew members. Even oxygen masks could cause skin irritation, holding in moisture and smoke. Despite these hazards, the equipment saved lives.

1st Lieutenant Stephen Ananian, pilot of the 339th Fighter Group based at Fowlmere in Cambridgeshire, takes a turn as 'flagman'.

At Fowlmere, P-51 Mustangs would take off from the grass runway two at a time and assemble to escort bombers on a mission. It was essential that all the aircraft were airborne as soon as possible in order to conserve fuel for the mission.

To speed up the process, the 339th placed an experienced fighter pilot at the side of the runway, signalling to each new pair of aeroplanes that it was safe for them to take off. As flagman, Stephen Ananian wore a colourful jacket and a white baseball cap so he could be easily spotted.

After the war Ananian became a photographer, later working on early digital processing. Today he lives in South Carolina, and he provided the information for this caption. If you visit The Eagle pub in Cambridge, look out for the '339' he burnt into their famous ceiling.

Colonel Lester Maitland sits at his desk at Boxted, Essex, in the summer of 1943.

Maitland was commanding officer of the 386th Bomb Group. The army censor who passed this print for publication has obscured the group's insignia behind him.

One of America's pioneering aviators, he was the first US pilot to fly at over 200mph. Along with his navigator Albert Helgenberger, Maitland completed the first ever trans-Pacific flight in June 1927 and, together with Helgenberger and Charles Lindbergh, was awarded the first Distinguished Flying Cross (DFC) for pushing the boundaries of manned flight.

When this photograph was taken, Maitland was the oldest commanding officer in the European Theater of Operations (ETO) and its oldest combat pilot. He would complete 44 missions and receive many awards, including his second DFC.

The great twist in Maitland's life came when he trained to be an Episcopal minister in the mid-1950s. He served the Iron River community in Michigan for many years. When asked why his life had taken such a turn he said, 'I watched the A-bomb and felt it could definitely destroy civilisation … The time to pray is now.'

Corporal Geraldine Hill of the Women's Army Corps, receives reports on aircraft positions in the plotting room of the 3rd Bomb Division at Elveden Hall, Suffolk. *(Overleaf)*

Hill lived in Texas all of her life and worked for more than 30 years as a bookkeeper for the Baptist General Convention of Texas. The war brought an interruption to her career when she volunteered as part of Dallas's civil defence and then when she enlisted in the Woman's Army Corps – a decision at which her boss 'nearly flipped'.

Hill served overseas for 27 months, not only in England, but in France, the Rhineland and Central Europe. After retirement she spent time fishing at the lakeside cottage she owned with her sister. Hill's nephew Don remembers her as 'an avid birder … [who] loved to go fishing. She was a quiet woman … [who] smiled often, with a kind nature.'

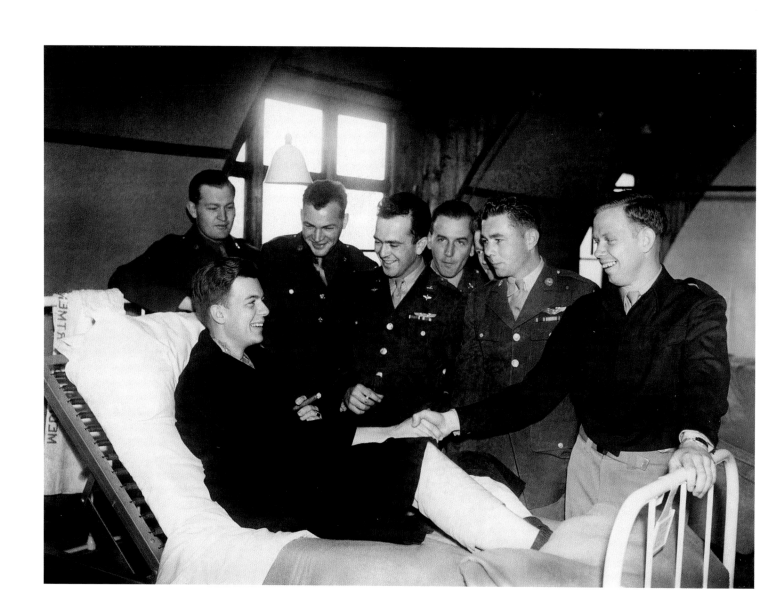

From his hospital bed, pilot Bill Whitson shakes the hand of bombardier, 1st Lieutenant Robert Barrall.

Two weeks before this photograph was taken, Barrall had helped Whitson fly their crippled B-17, 'Old Bill', back to base. Other crew members are gathered around his bedside.

The crew were flying a bombing mission over Heligoland, northern Germany, when they came under attack from Luftwaffe fighters. Barrall was wounded, along with both pilots and the top turret gunner, and the navigator was killed.

In this chaotic situation, the remaining able crew members took a turn at the flight controls and together managed to fly the aircraft back to Chelveston in Northamptonshire. They made an emergency landing with no working brakes or flaps to slow the bomber down.

Whitson and Barrall were awarded the Distinguished Service Cross (DSC) for their courage under extreme pressure. Just a month later, Barrall was killed in a mid-air collision with an RAF aircraft on a night training mission, leaving behind a fiancée. Bill Whitson, when asked in later life how he had handled the fear, said that rather than think about it 'you just get up in the morning and do what you're supposed to do'.

Navigator, 1st Lieutenant Daniel McColl enjoys a beer in the bar at Molesworth, Cambridgeshire.

The navigator's role was to direct the B-17 from departure to destination and back again. He needed a combination of good mathematical ability, navigational skill and concentration to maintain an accurate reckoning of the aeroplane's position at all times.

McColl was aged 27 when this photo was taken, the son of a Republican state senator. He was married and had a one-year-old son at home in Idaho. He was serving in the 303rd Bomb Group when he was killed on 14 May 1943 while on a mission to Kiel in Germany. His aircraft went into a spin and came down in the North Sea. After his death, his wife Virginia worked in the local Safeway supermarket. Five years later, she remarried.

American airmen are photographed enjoying a drink in an English pub by Private Alexander 'Cal' Sloan.

A lot of the interaction with local people took place over a 'bitter' or a 'mild'. Evidence of this is still common in East Anglian country pubs today, in the mementos, photographs and graffiti which adorn their walls.

The US official guidance to American servicemen included tips on how to behave in the pub, as well as cautionary advice: 'The British are beer-drinkers – and can hold it. The beer is now below peacetime strength, but can still make a man's tongue wag at both ends.'

Sloan served with the 1066th Signal Company based at Steeple Morden, Cambridgeshire. A keen photographer before the war, he was in possession of a Zeiss Contax 35mm camera, one of the most advanced models of the late 1930s. Soon after arriving at Steeple Morden, Sloan's wife sent him the camera, allowing him to build up a substantial record of his time in England.

Adelaide Grima Johnson, an American Red Cross worker from New York, August 1942.

Among the first contingent of the American Red Cross (ARC) to arrive in Britain, Johnson spent time stationed at the Milestone Club. Overlooking Kensington Park in London, it was somewhere American personnel on leave could eat, sleep and enjoy themselves.

In November 1944, Johnson represented the ARC at a conference with the French Ministry of Deportees, Refugees and Prisoners to discuss the logistics of rehabilitation. Johnson wrote, in a memorandum following the conference, that former prisoners held in a camp just outside Paris had lost patience with their repatriation, broken out and were annoying the locals with their vagrancy.

Johnson returned to New York in August 1945. She came from a wealthy family who had travelled frequently before the war between their homes in New York and Paris. She continued to travel to Paris after the war and married Comte Alain Eudes D'Eudeville, becoming the Comtesse D'Eudeville. She died in 2005, outliving her husband by 48 years.

Captain Roland Scott of the 322nd Bomb Group visits Edinburgh Castle during leave in 1943.

Many servicemen took advantage of their leave to sightsee in Britain. Roland Scott, from Macon, Georgia, was the younger brother of fighter ace Colonel Robert Lee Scott Jr. He had followed his brother into the service, becoming a pilot in 1933. While Robert was leading the Flying Tigers in China in 1942, Roland was appointed commander of the 450th Bomb Squadron, where he oversaw the training of crews flying B-26 Marauders.

On 14 May 1943, Roland Scott was lead pilot on his unit's first combat mission, over Ijmuiden in Holland. Shortly after bombing the target, the cockpit of Scott's aircraft was hit by 20mm cannon shell and the aircraft spun out of control. Shrapnel from the blast hit him in the chest, and he lost an eye in the explosion: 'I thought my face had been shot away, but I could see just enough with one eye to get up and hold the aircraft.' He was admitted to the 2nd General Hospital at Headington in Oxfordshire.

Scott retired in 1947. His son Roland Scott Jr was born in 1944 and also became a pilot, flying helicopters for the US Marine Corps during the Vietnam War.

Major General Frederick Anderson, commanding general of VIII Bomber Command, broadcasts to an American audience from the BBC's Broadcasting House in London.

Anderson's broadcast went out on the Blue Network, the predecessor of the American Broadcasting Company (ABC). It was December 1943 and the message of this particular broadcast was that 'operations made by USAAF last month were on a scale equal to major land and naval engagements'.

The bomber crews and fighter pilots had taken a battering over the previous few months and, as news of casualties and missing crews filtered back to the United States, it was important for the commanders to reiterate the strategic importance of the struggle taking place in the skies over Europe.

While some broadcasts were designed to keep Americans informed of military affairs, others aimed to strengthen the idea of shared wartime experience. The BBC's weekly show *Transatlantic Call – People to People* aired interviews with Brits and Americans describing their lives, in the hope that listeners would recognise mutual concerns.

John Havener, known as Jack, reads in bed. *(Overleaf)*

Havener flew B-26 Marauders with the 344th Bomb Group, based at Stansted Mountfitchet, Essex, in 1944. Covering 3,000 acres, it was the largest Ninth Air Force base in East Anglia and after the war became an international airport. The home-made night stands, racks and shelving, constructed from empty ammo boxes, helped make his hut feel more like home.

Havener completed 68 combat missions in the medium bombers, many of them from Stansted, and was awarded the Distinguished Flying Cross (DFC) – given to American airmen who showed 'heroism or extraordinary achievement while participating in aerial flight'.

Havener grew up in Illinois and worked his entire adult life for the International Harvester Company, an agricultural equipment supplier. After the war he remained in the active reserve of the USAAF, rising to Lieutenant Colonel. He was one of the founding members of IWM Duxford's American Air Museum.

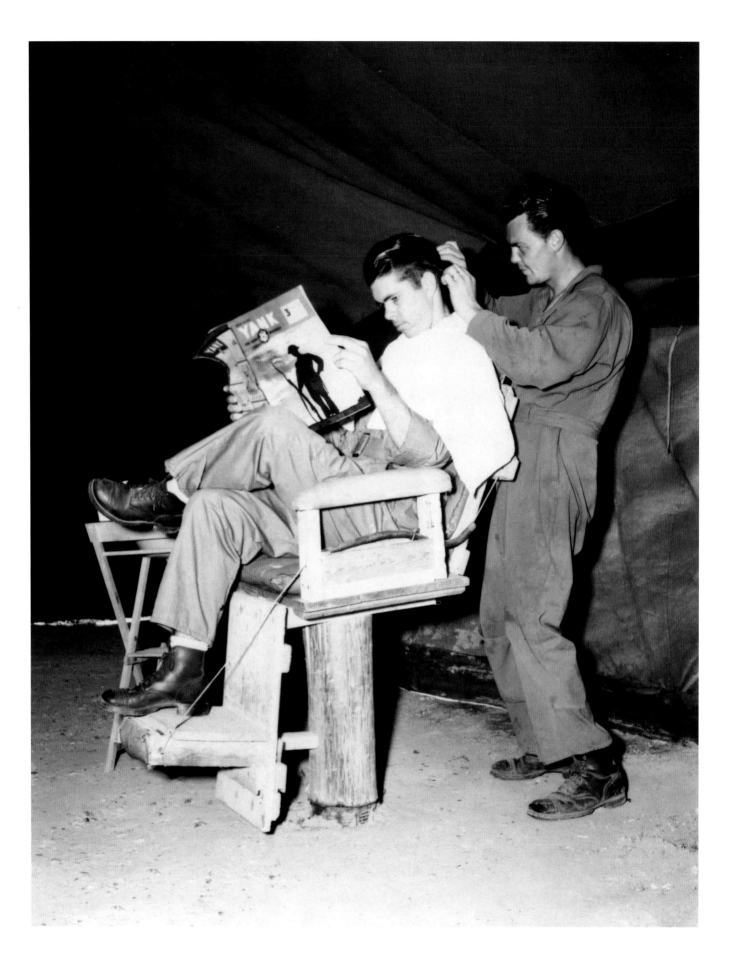

Private Oscar Burns cuts the hair of Private Lloyd Yates in a makeshift chair they designed and built together, August 1943.

The photograph's original press caption stated that 'even in the combat zone officers and men must give a thought to their personal appearance: long hair and unshaven faces are not tolerated. In the absences of adequate civilian barber facilities, squadrons have set up their own shops … Most of the men, however, shave themselves – and in cold water.'

Burns was a private in the 386th Bomb Group, which flew B-26 Marauders from Boxted and Great Dunmow in Essex. He held the lowest rank among enlisted men, and it is difficult to build a detailed picture of his war. Most memoirs and records focus on the history of flying or senior administrative personnel.

However, official records show that Burns was the son of a logger from Tennessee, who had a rocky childhood resulting in a conviction for auto theft in 1939, three years before he joined the USAAF. His enlistment record classes his pre-war job as 'semi-skilled chauffeur or driver'. After the war he returned to Washington state and, eventually, to prison. In 1969 – two years before his death – he was sentenced to 15 years for grand larceny. This was probably the final entry on what the prosecutor described as 'a long prior record'.

Sergeant Albert Krassman Jr stands before his handiwork on the B-24, 'Kentucky Bell'.

Born in Colorado, Krassman enlisted in 1943 and served as ground crew with the 446th Bomb Group, based at Bungay in Suffolk. He worked as a gunsight, turret and armour mechanic, referring to himself playfully as a 'bomb-stuffer-inner'. His crucial work helped maintain the B-24s for combat missions.

Senior personnel turned a blind eye to the unofficial nose art which adorned many American planes. It allowed crews to form and express a sense of identity. It could also be an outlet for superstition, with airmen claiming it gave them something to pat for luck before and after missions.

Krassman painted nose art on many of the 446th Bomb Group aircraft. His subjects included scantily-clad women, cartoon characters and the plane names themselves. Such images were usual for USAAF crews who also decorated aircraft with song titles, puns and even depictions of wives or girlfriends left behind.

Private First Class Barbara O'Brien applies the finishing touches to a skull on the nose of a B-26 Marauder.

O'Brien enlisted in Dallas, Texas, in December 1942. At the time this photograph was taken a year later, she was part of a Women's Army Corps unit based at Marks Hall, Essex, which had taken over from the British WAAF the duties of plotting, typing and stenography.

O'Brien worked as a plotter and moved with her unit to France, and finally to Bad Kissingen in Germany. As a talented artist, she was in demand with the flyboys to add nose art to their aircraft. The aircraft she is painting here, the 'Jolly Roger' (41-34942), belonged to the 323rd Bomb Group, based at nearby Earls Colne in Essex.

After the war she attended art school in San Miguel de Allende, Mexico. It was there she met her husband of 51 years, Frank Kuzel, who was himself a veteran – he had been part of the 101st Airborne Division and a prisoner of war in Germany. They later returned to the USA and brought up two sons in Dallas, both of whom served in the military.

1st Lieutenant Frank Oiler, pilot (right), with Staff Sergeant Donald Shupe, ground crew, in front of P-51 Mustang 'Sherman Was Right' at Duxford, Cambridgeshire.

Ohio-born Oiler enlisted in October 1942. The first time he used his guns, the squadron commander likened his effectiveness to taking on the enemy with a squash racket. His P-47 Thunderbolt was named 'Eileen', after his wife, and sported an aggressive wasp as nose art.

In December 1944 the 78th Fighter Group transferred to P-51D Mustangs, which were faster and had a better heating system. Oiler also recalled a further benefit: 'North American Aviation ... added a relief tube for those long, long missions. You were okay as long as the tube didn't freeze up on you. If it did, you'd have a long, wet ride!'

Donald Shupe grew up in a Mormon family in Salt Lake City, Utah. After the war, he returned to a career as an auto mechanic.

The name 'Sherman Was Right', on the aircraft which replaced 'Eileen', originates from a quote which Oiler attributed to the American Civil War general, William Tecumseh Sherman: 'There is many a boy here who looks on war as all glory, but, boys, it is all hell!'

Sergeant Russell Butts (left) and Sergeant Robert Sand, ground crew of the 55th Fighter Group, pretend to light the fuse on a 500-pound bomb, July 1944.

Robert Sand was responsible for the maintenance and repair of fighter aircraft. As a specialist in propeller mechanics, Sand performed a crucial role in ensuring that the engine was running correctly and would feel personally accountable for the safe return of the aircraft he worked on, saying he 'could not rest easy until every ship was off safely, and had returned safely. And when any ship was lost unaccountably, there remained a little nagging question.'

Ground personnel sought distractions while waiting for their aircraft to come back. Armed with his camera, Sand made a photographic record of the sights and antics on base. This photograph was taken on Independence Day 1944. He was also a keen artist, and painted the nose art on several famous fighter planes. On his retirement in 1991, he painted one final piece of nose art – on his wife's wheelbarrow!

Lieutenant Colonel Louis Houck dons his 'devil's helmet' prior to a mission. *(Overleaf)*

Houck, from North Carolina, enlisted in July 1940 and served as a pilot with the 365th Fighter Group of the Ninth Air Force, also known as the 'Hell Hawks'. He was commander of the 387th Squadron from May 1943 until October 1944.

Perhaps appropriately, Houck wore his customised devil's helmet on missions over Europe, flying his P-47 'Screamin' Weemie'. The nose art of his plane depicted a demon brandishing a pitchfork. Despite his extravagant appearance he was described by a group member as 'quiet', 'introverted' and 'respected'.

In 1944 Houck was responsible for almost entirely destroying a retreating German convoy in France. The convoy had been transporting gasoline and ammunition and its smoking wreckage was captured on camera shortly afterwards.

Lieutenant Donald Emerson of the 4th Fighter Group, holds a rabbit's foot talisman, which he wears on a chain around his neck.

A North Dakota farm-boy, Emerson flew a P-51 Mustang named 'Fighting Donald', with nose art depicting Donald Duck. His rabbit foot talisman was a gift from his girlfriend, Elinor, to bring good luck on missions. Airmen were often highly superstitious or ritualistic, putting their clothes and equipment on in exactly the same order as the previous mission.

Unfortunately, the talisman let Emerson down. Returning from an escort mission to Kessel, Germany, Emerson became separated from the section he was leading. He successfully fought off six German fighters, of which he shot down two. With no ammunition left, Emerson flew low in heavy cloud and transmitted that he was 'on the deck and heading home'. His comrades could hear him, but could not find him. Enemy flak shot him down and he crashed in Belgium in territory held by the British. It was 25 December 1944.

Crew Chief Glesner Weckbacher reportedly refused to take part in the Christmas celebrations as he sat in the dark waiting for his pilot to return.

Sergeant William 'Bill' Pulliam of the 91st Bomb Group holding his cat, Cross-Eyes.

Bill Pulliam was from Kansas City, Missouri. He enlisted in 1942 and joined the 91st Bomb Group, where he worked as photographer for the 401st Bomb Squadron at Bassingbourn, Cambridgeshire. Pulliam was responsible for loading strike cameras into B-17 Flying Fortresses, which would photograph bombs falling on the target. The images would later be analysed by intelligence officers to judge the success of the mission.

If an aircraft from Pulliam's unit landed at the wrong base, it was his job to retrieve the film. On Christmas Eve 1944, bad weather prevented several Fortresses from returning to base, and Pulliam was sent 70 miles with his colleague Sergeant Joseph Harlick to prepare the aircraft for their next raid. Driving at midnight with blacked out headlights, Pulliam and Harlick collided with an unexploded bomb which had been dropped from an ammunition truck. Fortunately the bomb failed to detonate and Pulliam returned home to Missouri at the end of the war, where he married his sweetheart Reyina in June 1945.

War artist Frank Beresford paints a B-17, closely observed by Lady Moe, 96th Bomb Group mascot.

A prolific artist, Beresford's works include 3,000 separate commissions, international tours and numerous royal portraits. During the Second World War, he served as an official war artist for the RAF, additionally producing works for the US forces stationed in Britain. He became only the second Briton to be awarded the Exceptional Service Award by the USAAF, the highest civilian honour.

Lady Moe was adopted by Captain Andrew Miracle's crew in Tunisia in August 1943 and transported back to their base at Snetterton Heath in Norfolk, via a raid on Bordeaux.

She became internationally famous as the 'Queen of the Heath', serving as a mascot in the Army-Navy football match in 1944 and appearing alongside the Queen at a charity event. Moe developed a taste for tobacco, toilet roll and doughnuts and became increasingly irascible. She remains the only known donkey to have flown a combat mission.

Lieutenants Allen Bryson, Sol Greenberg and Albert Gehrt of the 453rd Bomb Group pose wearing flying helmets, underwear and parachute harnesses. *(Overleaf)*

Bryson, Greenberg and Gehrt were the pilot, navigator and bombardier of B-24 Liberator 'The Gypsy Queen'. By Christmas 1944, they had completed 21 missions together, flying from their base at Old Buckenham, Norfolk.

Despite the light-heartedness of this photograph, their final missions would be some of their most difficult. Greenberg described his crew's penultimate mission to bomb the bridge at Remagen, Germany, on 29 December as particularly depressing, claiming 'I am as miserable as I physically can be'.

The crew found the bridge at Remagen covered by thick cloud and, despite releasing their bombs, returned home disheartened. 'We know we have missed', Greenberg reported. While the mission may have been a failure, Bryson, Greenberg and Gehrt completed their tour of duty two days later and returned home to the United States.

Captain Edwin Caudill, Group Adjutant at the 4th Fighter Group's air base in Debden, Essex, takes some time out from his official duties to practice archery.

An adjutant was responsible for various aspects of administration on the air base, including handling official correspondence, distributing orders and maintaining records. Each squadron had its own adjutant, but Caudill was assigned to the group's headquarters.

Caudill came from Kentucky and remained in the Air Force after the Second World War, serving in Korea and Vietnam and finishing his career as a colonel. His post-military career was in business studies and college administration. He remained a keen hunter all his life.

Technical Sergeant Francis Burns poses with an accordion in one of a series of press photographs of the 303rd Bomb Group, intended to reveal the lighter side of base life.

From Somerville, Massachusetts, Burns served as a radio operator with the 303rd Bomb Group, known as the 'Hell's Angels' and stationed at Molesworth in Cambridgeshire. Burns flew almost exclusively with Captain Carl Morales's crew in B-17 'Sky Wolf'. He had completed 14 missions when this photograph was taken.

On 13 June 1943, he completed his quota of 25 missions. The pilot, 1st Lieutenant James McDonald, flew in low and dropped a large towel. He later explained that, as this was their final mission, he was literally throwing in the towel.

Captain Alexander 'Stormy' Sadowski prepares to write a letter home, February 1944.

'Stormy' was a weather officer with the 56th Fighter Group. His job was to provide a weather forecast ahead of each mission and monitor conditions for landing when pilots returned. If the weather was particularly bad, he would issue a warning that 'oranges are sour' over the radio, which meant that returning pilots should not attempt a landing at their home airfield.

Stormy was always the last person to talk to assembled pilots at their mission briefing. One wrote to Roger Freeman that Stormy usually 'concluded with a joke or some kind of levity to send the fighters out of the mission hut with smiles on their faces and, occasionally, with laughter – to relax them before they went to their planes'.

Here in his bedroom at Halesworth, Suffolk, he writes his daily letter home to his wife Helena, whose portrait is believed to be the one visible behind him. They were married until her death in 1979 and had four children. Stormy continued a career in meteorology in civilian life, publishing many technical papers and articles on subjects such as tornados and pollution.

Frieda Wilkinson receives a clock from Brigadier General Murray Woodbury and Staff Sergeant Ismael Bose of the 78th Fighter Group at Duxford, Cambridgeshire. *(Overleaf)*

Frieda, an Air Raid Precautions (ARP) Warden, was the British wife of fighter pilot Captain James Wilkinson, commanding officer of the 82nd Fighter Squadron. An accomplished fighter ace, Wilkinson was flying his P-47 Thunderbolt on a practice mission when bad weather caused him to crash into a mountainside in Llandovery, Wales, on 4 June 1944.

He was posthumously awarded the Distinguished Service Cross (DSC) and Silver Star for gallantry, which Frieda received on his behalf. She was also presented with a clock made by Bose, her husband's crew chief, who told press at the ceremony, 'it's just a little remembrance for the wife of the finest pilot our squadron ever had'.

Frieda struggled to get over the death of her husband. She killed herself six months later. Reports noted that there was a portrait of her husband by her side.

Brothers, 2nd Lieutenant Clifford McIlveen (left) and 1st Lieutenant Clarence McIlveen pose for a press photographer, October 1943.

Clifford and Clarence McIlveen grew up in Oregon. They were separated after enlisting, but coincidence reunited them when both were assigned to the 385th Bomb Group at Great Ashfield, Suffolk. Clifford, the younger brother at 22, was first to arrive in the European Theater of Operations (ETO), flying as a co-pilot on bombing missions.

However, their reunion was short-lived. Soon afterwards Clifford was shot down and taken prisoner of war at Stalag Luft I, where he remained until 1945. He returned home to marry and have two children, but he never saw his brother again. Clarence and his crew were shot down on a bombing mission over Rostock on 24 February 1944 – his 26th birthday. His body was never recovered.

Clifford joined the 190th Fighter Squadron, Idaho Air National Guard, in the Korean War. He died, aged 29, in a training accident near Waco Airport, Texas, in 1952.

Left to right: Brothers, Henry, Barney and Thomas Smith at home in the United States shortly after the war.

The youngest brother, Henry, enlisted in 1942 and served with an armored division. Barney served in Guam with the 20th Air Force.

Thomas, the eldest brother, enlisted in 1941 and flew with the 359th Fighter Group. On 11 April 1944, returning from an escort mission, he crash-landed his P-47 in France, later reporting that 'I was either hit and lost gas or used more than I expected as I ran out ...'.

After landing, Thomas spent five months in France, evading capture with the help of a French family. Unfortunately, while attempting to get back to the UK, he was captured and imprisoned. When the Germans tried to move him and his fellow prisoners away from the advancing Allied armies, he escaped and returned to England. He died in 2001, aged 83.

Lieutenant George Hartman (left) and Lieutenant Robert Belliveau read *Yank: the Army Weekly* at Duxford, August 1943.

Both Hartman and Belliveau were pilots with the 78th Fighter Group which flew out of Duxford in Cambridgeshire, primarily in P-47 Thunderbolts. For the last few months of the war the P-47s were replaced by P-51 Mustangs, which had a longer range.

Belliveau flew 96 missions and survived the war. Hartman was not so lucky. An eyewitness account by another pilot described the moment his P-47 was attacked by German aircraft returning from a mission over La Rochelle, France, in January 1944: 'I made another 360 degree tight turn at 9,000 feet and saw Lieutenant Hartman's ship going down in a wide spiral while two enemy aircraft circled around his plane ... I could not see a 'chute ... I looked back and observed a tall column of black smoke, which was probably Lieutenant Hartman's ship burning.'

Left to right: Best man Gene Hammerick, Robert and May Kirschner, bridesmaid Alice Fuller, and May's parents Harold and Rose Lockwood, photographed at St Mary's Church, Coddenham, Suffolk, November 1943.

While the end of the war meant a welcome return to home for many, for others it was the beginning of a new chapter of life.

May Rose Lockwood was crowned May Queen of her village aged 14 and joined the Women's Land Army in 1940. She met Robert Kirschner, who was working in a service squadron with the nearby 56th Fighter Group, and they married in 1943. Shortly after the war ended, she was one of many thousands of young women who left their families and friends behind to begin a new life in America. With her baby daughter and husband, she settled in Syracuse, New York, and worked as a nanny. The couple were married for 51 years.

PICTURE CREDITS AND DATES

p.7 (FRE 13671)

p.8 (FRE 12776)
10 (Image courtesy of Mark Copeland)

p.12 (FRE 9782)
Brigadier General Robert Candee
(1892–1963)
Air Vice-Marshal John H 'Albiac
(1894–1963)

p.14 (FRE 4417)
1st Lieutenant Immanuel 'Manny'
Klette (1918–1988)

p.16 (FRE 4792)
Lieutenant Oswald Masoni
(1923–1988)

p.18 (FRE 3517)
Captain Clark Gable (1901–1960)
Sergeant Phil Hulse (1923–)
Sergeant Kenneth Huls (1919–2009)

p. 20 (FRE 9781)
King George VI (1895–1952)
Queen Elizabeth (1900–2002)
Princess Elizabeth (1926–)
Major General James 'Jimmy' Doolittle
(1896–1993)
Major Lloyd Mason (1916–1987)

p.22 (FRE 9839)
Major William Wyler (1902–1981)
Terence Rattigan (1911–1977)

p.24 (FRE 266)
Major Jesse Davis (1915–1964)

p.26 (FRE 5854) © Albert T. Keeler
Peter Brame (1931–)

p.28 (FRE 1935)
Janet Townshend (1937–1997)
Tessa Grant (1936–2015)
Gloria Grant (1937–1965)

p.30 (FRE 6556)
Margaret Holley (1924–2002)

p.32 (FRE 10643)
William Glasscock (1902–1984)
Pearl Glasscock (1929–)

p.34 (FRE 13074) © Robert Sand
Jan Houston Monaghan (1917–2006)

p.36 (FRE 13674)
Corporal Joseph Sleeping Bear
(1924–1997)

p.38 (FRE 280)
1st Lieutenant Stanley Markusen
(1917–1997)
Major Charles Clapp Jr (1899–1957)
William Randolph Hearst Jr (1908–1993)
Major John DuFour (1909–1993)

p.40 (FRE 2552)
Frederick Christensen Jr (1921–2006)

p.42 (FRE 9553)
Lieutenant Edwin Wright (1925–1959)

p.44 (FRE 4155)
Staff Sergeant Richard Grimm
(1924–1999)

p.46 (FRE 888)
Lieutenant Harry Erickson (1920–1998)

p.48 (FRE 1152)
Technical Sergeant Robert Siavage
(1920–1988)

p.50 (FRE 987)
Staff Sergeant Ward W Kirkpatrick
(1923–1943)

p.52 (FRE 1342)
Staff Sergeant Richard 'Slug' Schultheis
(1923–2011)

p.54 (FRE 4796)
Sergeant Leo Teetman Jr (1923–2000)

p.56 (FRE 14280)
Staff Sergeant Jayson Smart
(1921–1997)

p.58 (FRE 9744)
Major General Carl Spaatz (1891–1974)
Major Charles Kegelman (1915–1945)

p.60 (FRE 9765)

p.62 (FRE 4067)
Corporal George Oelkers (1920–2008)

p.64 (FRE 9342)
Lieutenant Gustave Binnebose
(1920–2004)
Chief Aviation Pilot James Chandler
(1921–2007)

p.66 (FRE 4071)
Staff Sergeant Elmer Leonard
(1920– 2004)

p.68 (FRE 340)
Virginia Irwin (1908–1980)
Lieutenant Glennon 'Bubbles' Moran
(1919–1986)

p.70 (FRE 3473)

p.72 (FRE 285)
Technical Sergeant Lester Reifeiss
(1918–1979)
Sergeant Jasper 'J D' Taylor (1920–1976)

p.74 (FRE 11675)

p.76 (FRE 10310)
Warrant Officer Cecil Broxton
(1919–1996)

p.78 (FRE 410)
Intelligence Officer Captain Gordon
Burris (1904–1963)

p.80 (FRE 1042)
Captain Jesse Barrett Jr (1900–1986)

p.82 (FRE 9741)
Major General Ira Eaker (1896–1987)

p.84 (FRE 11690)
Lieutenant John Gerber (1919–2005)

SOURCES

Key sources for our research are listed below.

General sources:

World War II Enlistment Records, National Archives
and Records Administration.
1900, 1910, 1920, 1930 and 1940 censuses.
www.findagrave.com
www.ancestry.com
www.fold3.com

FRE 9782
www.afhra.af.mil
www.raf.mod.uk/history

FRE 4417
The Man Who Wouldn't Quit: The Manny Klette Biography,
Roger A Freeman (91st Bomb Group Memorial Association, n.d.)
www.8thafhsoregon.com/archive/306th/306th-BG-Combat-Crews-08.pdf

FRE 4792
The Mighty Eighth War Diary, Roger A Freeman (London: Arms and
Armour, revised edition, 1990).
www.bbc.co.uk/history/ww2peopleswar/stories/77/a5068677.shtml
www.joebaugher.com

FRE 3517
www.dearmrgable.com/?page_id=3070
Clark Gable, in Pictures: Candid Images of the Actor's Life, Chrystopher J
Spicer (Jefferson, NC: McFarland & Co, 2012).
Clark Gable: Biography, Filmography, Bibliography, Chrystopher J Spicer
(Jefferson, NC: McFarland & Co, 2001).

FRE 9781
Shades of Kimbolton: A Narrative of the 379th Bombardment Group,
Derwyn D Robb (San Angelo, TX: Newsfoto Pub Co, 1946).
Greenly Daily Tribune, 17 Nov 1944.

FRE 9839
'Looking for Flying Officer Rattigan', Group Captain Clive Montellier RA,
Terence Rattigan Society.
*William Wyler: The Life and Films of Hollywood's Most Celebrated
Director*, Gabriel Miller (Lexington, KY: University Press of Kentucky, 2013).
This is England: British Film and the People's War, 1939-1945,
Neil Rattigan (Cranbury, NJ: Associated University Presses, 2001).

FRE 266
Duxford Diary, 1942–1945, Bowen I Hosford, ed. (W Heffer & Sons Ltd,
Cambridge, 1945).
Records of 78th Fighter Group USAAF at Duxford, 1943–1945, IWM.
IWM Documents Archive, Documents.10395.
'Lt. Col. Davis shoots his wife, then kills himself', Herb Pasik, *Redlands
Daily Facts*, 12 October 1964.

FRE 5854
Rich Relations: The American Occupation of Britain 1942-1945,
David Reynolds (London: Phoenix Press, 2000).
www.ww2color.com/search/webapps/slides/slides
php?action=update&primary_key=11903 www.8theast.org/children/

FRE 1935
www.norfolksamericanconnections.com/the-friendly-invasion/
www.familynotices24.co.uk/edp/view/787068/janet-hopton
www.466thbga.com/466th-bomb-group-news.php
Air Force Fifty: 50 Years USAF. A Look at the Air Force, Air Force
Association and Commemorative Las Vegas Reunion, Air Force
Association (Paducah, KY: Turner Pub Co, 1998).

FRE 6556
'President Tyler Docks with British War Brides', *Chicago Tribune*, 2 April 1946.
'Minutes of the 895th public hearings and regular meeting held by the
City Planning Commission of the City of Livonia', www.ci.livonia.mi.us
Eighth Air Force: The American Bomber Crews in Britain, Donald L Miller
(London: Aurum, 2007).

FRE 10643
Ashwell Museum, www.ashwellmuseum.org.uk
'No Silver Lining', Pearl Williams (nee Glasscock), www.ancestry.co.uk

FRE 13074
Notes written by Robert Sand in the Roger Freeman Collection,
IWM Obituary, *The Greeley Tribune*, 12 August 2006.
www.armyairforces.com

FRE 13674
Snetterton Falcons: The 96th Bomb Group in World War II, Robert E
Doherty and Geoffrey D Ward (Dallas, TX: Taylor, 1989).
Toward a New Era in Indian Affairs: American Indians and World War II,
Alison R Bernstein (Norman: University of Oklahoma Press, 1991).

FRE 280
*US Eighth Air Force and its British World War II hosts: A History of
International Public Relations*, Kerry Anderson Crooks (Gainesville,
FL: University of Florida, 1999).
William Randolph Hearst Jr Obituary, Bruce Lambert, *New York Times*,
16 May 1993.

FRE 2552
The 'Connection' in East Tennessee, Olga Jones Edwards and Izora
Waters Frizzell (Johnson City, TN: The Overmountain Press, 2001).
Washington State Institution Records (Corrections Department,
Reformatory, Admissions Registers, 1908-1923).
'Well known logger dies at Humptulips', *Denning Prospector*, 6 February 1925.

Spokane Daily Chronicle, 15 October 1969.
Death notice, *Walla Walla Union Bulletin*, 8 February 1971.

FRE 9553
Leap Off: 404th Fighter Group Combat History, Andrew F Wilson, ed.
(San Angelo, TX: Newsfoto Pub Co, 1950).
North Carolina Death Certificates.

FRE 4155
www.303rdbg.com
www.306bg.us/Echoes%20files/92apr172.pdf

FRE 888
Journal of Lieutenant Ben H Rushing.
www.wwiimemorial.com

FRE 1152
Social Security Death Index.
First Over Germany: A History of the 306th Bombardment Group, Russell
A Strong (Winston-Salem, NC: Hunter Print Co, 1982).

FRE 987
www.303rdbg.com/missionreports/036.pdf
www.jugglinghandgrenades.blogspot.co.uk/2011_07_01_archive.html

FRE 1342
Obituary, John J Lopatich Funeral Home, 17 April 2011.

FRE 4796
www.384thbombgroup.com
Obituary, www.usgennet.org
Obituary of Mary T Teetman (Sergeant Leo Teetman Jr's wife),
Spinelli-Ricciuti Funeral Home, 31 December 2013.

FRE 14280
The Mighty Eighth War Diary, Roger A Freeman (London: Arms and
Armour, revised edition, 1990).
www.americanairmuseum.com/mission/1701

FRE 9744
www.af.mil
www.unz.org/Pub/Yank-1942aug19-00005:5

FRE 9765
www.303rdbg.com/missionreports/092.pdf
Brooklyn Eagle, 11 February 1944

FRE 4067
Obituary, Lawrence E Young Funeral Home, 2008.
The Story of the 390th Bomb Group, Albert E Milliken, ed. (Privately
printed: The Story of the 390th Bomb Group, Inc., 1947).

FRE 9342
www.heritageleague.org/Journals/2002iii%20Fall.pdf
www.southwestairfields.co.uk/?page_id=53

FRE 4071
Obituary, *Hartford Courant*, 6 May 2004.
www.390thspace.com

FRE 340
Private papers of Virginia Irwin.
'Glennon Moran – Granite City Ace', Virginia Irwin, *St. Louis
Post-Dispatch*, 1945.
www.veterantributes.org
'A Look Back: P-D reporter who reached Berlin blocked by Army censors',
Tim O'Neil, *St. Louis Post-Dispatch*, 8 May 2011.

FRE 3473
When Jim Crow Met John Bull, Graham Smith (St. Martin's Press, NY, 1988).
Eighth in the East learning resource pack.
Eighth Air Force: The American Bomber Crews in Britain, Donald L Miller
(London: Aurum, 2007).

FRE 285
Obituary of Bertha Delpha Bessemer (Sergeant Taylor's sister),
Hart-Wyatt funeral home, 13 May 2012.

FRE 11675
Popular Science, December 1943.
http://hansard.millbanksystems.com/
www.flightglobal.com

FRE 410
The Billboard, 4 March 1944.
Evening Independent, Massillon, Ohio, 3 February 1948.

FRE 1042
www.303rdbg.com/rost-ab.html
The S-2 Story, Lieutenant Carlton M Smith. Available as part of this
mission report: www.303rdbg.com/missionreports/129.pdf

FRE 9741
Obituary, *New York Times*, 8 August 1987.
www.af.mil
*Air Power. From Kitty Hawk to Gulf War II: a History of the People,
Ideas and Machines that Transformed War in the Century of Flight*,
Stephen Budiansky (London: Viking, 2003).

FRE 11690
www.wwiiaircraftperformance.org/mustang/scouting-force.html
www.genlookups.com/nm/webbbs_config.pl/noframes/read/263
www.littlefriends.co.uk/gallery.php?Group=sf&Style=item&-origStyle=list
&Item=85&Temp=1824&searchString=

FRE 955
Obituary, *Chicago Tribune*, 5 February 1988.
www.303rdbg.com
*Air Force Chaplains, Vol. 1. The Service of Chaplains to Army Air Units,
1917-1946*, Daniel B Jorgensen (Washington DC: Office of the Chief of
Air Force Chaplains, 1961).

FRE 4782
The American Airman in Europe, Roger A Freeman (London: Arms and Armour Press, 1991).
'Over Here': The GIs in Wartime Britain, Juliet Gardiner (London: Collins and Brown, 1992).

FRE 2485
Obituary, *Brooklyn Eagle*, 4 June 1954.
Wolfpack Warriors: The Story of World War II's Most Successful Fighter Outfit, Roger A Freeman (London : Grub Street, 2004).
Gabby: A Fighter Pilot's Life, Francis Gabreski and Carl Molesworth (Atglen, PA: Schiffer Pub, 1998).

FRE 45
www.4thfightergroupassociation.org
Obituary, *St. Louis Post-Dispatch*, 1 September 1993.

FRE 1026
Correspondence with Gary Moncur of the 303rd Bomb Group Association.
Rock Island National Cemetery database.

FRE 4159
www.303rdbga.com/pp-fleming-dressing-for-mission.html
www.newspapers.com/image/82644721/?terms=William%2BW%2BFleming
'Over Here': The GIs in Wartime Britain, Juliet Gardiner (London: Collins and Brown, 1992).
Eighth Air Force: The American Bomber Crews in Britain, Donald L Miller (London: Aurum, 2007).

FRE 5998
Email correspondence with Stephen Ananian.

FRE 7789
www.wisconsinaviationhalloffame.org
Obituary, *New York Times*, 30 March 1990.
'Lester Maitland Is Finding Peace of Mind in Switch from "General" to "Reverend"', *Milwaukee Journal*, 19 March 1957.
'Priest Vows Taken By Lester Maitland', *Milwaukee Journal*, 12 July 1957.

FRE 10468
www.facebook.com/mighty8thmuseum/posts/10152661921760797
www.texashistory.unt.edu
www.aviation-safety.net

FRE 983
MACR (Missing Air Crew Report) 15593.
Tarkio Avalanche, 28 May 1943.
Idaho Statesman, 22 Nov 2008.

FRE 10542
United States War Department, Instructions for American Servicemen in Britain, 1942.
www.ww2color.com/about.php

Rich Relations: The American Occupation of Britain 1942-1945, David Reynolds (London: Phoenix Press, 2000).
'Over Here': The GIs in Wartime Britain, Juliet Gardiner (London: Collins and Brown, 1992).

FRE 13655
WWII European Theatre Monographs, 494A French Rehabilitation, American Red Cross.
Brooklyn Daily Eagle, 22 January 1936.
New York Passenger Lists.

FRE 7503
The Ijmuiden Power plant raids of WWII, Airpower Misapplied, Air Command and Staff College Student Report, Major James N Openshaw.
B-26 Marauder At War, Roger A Freeman (New York: Scribner, 1978).
The Mighty Eighth in Colour, Roger A Freeman (London: Arms and Armour, 1991).

FRE 9792
www.afhra.af.mil
www.raf.mod.uk/history
www.oac.cdlib.org
LIFE magazine, 16 October 1944.
Network Nations: A Transnational History of British and American Broadcasting, Michele Hilmes (London: Routledge, 2012).
http://genome.ch.bbc.co.uk/

FRE 7134
Obituary, Dignity Memorial, Memphis Funeral Home, 16 May 2011, www.dignitymemorial.com
The Distinguished Flying Cross Society, Randy W Baumgardner (Paducah, KY: Turner Pub Co, 2004).

FRE 2252
Obituary, *Boston Globe*, 10 April 2006.
Obituary, *Washington Post*, 14 April 2006.
America's Top Eighth Air Force Aces in Their Own Words, William Hess (St Paul, MN: MBI Pub Co, 2001).

FRE 7671
www.aviationmuseum.net/446BGimagesAK.html
Obituary of Sergeant Albert Krassman Jr, www.legacy.com/obituaries/pasadenastarnews/obituary.aspx?n=albert-krassman&pid=19374842
Eighth Air Force: The American Bomber Crews in Britain, Donald L Miller (London: Aurum, 2007).
Norfolk and Suffolk Aviation Museum.

FRE 13539
Obituary, Hughes Crown Hill Funeral Home, 2013.
www.kathyamen.net/journal/jroger.htm
B-26 Marauder at War, Roger A Freeman (New York: Scribner, 1978).
US 9th Air Force Bases In Essex, 1943-44, Martin W Bowman (London: Pen and Sword, 2010).
www.britishpathe.com/video/ww2-operations-control-centre http://collections.uakron.edu/cdm/ref/collection/p15960coll3/id/1392/

FRE 5603
The Fight in the Clouds: The Extraordinary Combat Experience of P-51 Mustang Pilots During World War II, James P Busha (Minneapolis, MN: Zenith Press, 2014).
Aces of the 78th Fighter Group, Thomas McKelvey Cleaver (Oxford: Osprey, 2013).
Obituary of Donald Shupe, *Deseret News*, 28 May 2000.

FRE 12873
Notes written by Robert Sand in the Roger Freeman Collection, IWM.

FRE 9803
Hell Hawks! The Untold Story of the American Fliers who Savaged Hitler's Wehrmacht, R F Dorr and T D Jones (Minneapolis: Zenith Press, 2010).
P-47 Thunderbolt Aces of the Ninth and Fifteenth Air Forces, J Scutts (Oxford: Osprey, 2003).
www.skylighters.org/potw/pow12082003.html

FRE 39
www.warbirdsresourcegroup.org/URG/emerson.html
www.preddy-foundation.org
www.airforce.togetherweserved.com

FRE 5671
www.91stbombgroup.com

FRE 3968
Lady Moe: Queen of the Heath: A Short Documentary, Alex Fryer,
www.youtube.com/watch?v=3ThJmJteh-s
www.westendatwar.org.uk/page_id__157.aspx
www.grantwatersfineart.co.uk/FrankBeresford.html

FRE 1868
The Mighty Eighth War Diary, Roger A Freeman (London: Arms and Armour, revised edition, 1990).
www.453rdbg.com/733rd%20Air%20Crews/Lt.%20Allan%20Bryson.html

FRE 3
www.4thfightergroupassociation.org
Obituary, *Salisbury Post*, 8 August 2012.

FRE 986
www.303rdbg.com/

FRE 2569
www.poles.org
Letter from Brigadier General E L Eubank supplied to Roger Freeman by FX Schuster, 2 May 1973.

FRE 14260
Delaware County Daily Times, 8 August 1944.
Duxford Diary, 1942–1945, Bowen I Hosford, ed. (W Heffer & Sons Ltd, Cambridge, 1945).
www.ulongbeach.com/James_Wilkinson_Accident_Page.html
Death Certificate, Frieda Wilkinson.

FRE 4960
www.abmc.gov
www.merkki.com/guestbook2003page1.htm

FRE 6181
T P Smith, 'A Five Month Evasion, Capture, and Escape as Captain Thomas P. Smith remembers...' archived by Char Baldridge, Historian, 359th Fighter Group Association, posted by Janet Fogg, co-author of *Fogg in the Cockpit*. Accessed via www.facebook.com
359th Fighter Group, Thomas H Raines, ed. (Norwich: The Soman-Wherry Press Ltd, 1945).
'Barney Smith', *Hartford Courant* Archives, 2 August 2003.
19th Bomb Group Roster Guam 1945, accessed via http://www.19thbg.org/

FRE 301
Veterans History Project oral history interview with Belliveau, Mariemont City Schools Legacy, http://legacy.mariemontschools.org/
Obituary of Lieutenant Robert Belliveau, *Cincinnati Enquirer*, 17 March 2009.
MACR 1741.

FRE 2509
Obituary, *Syracuse Post Standard*, 11 July 2012.
56th Fighter Group unit history.
www.locategrave.org